Surviving Kidney Disease

The Essential Guide to Managing Chronic Renal Failure

Isabella White

Copyright © 2023 by Isabella White.

__Disclaimer:__ The information contained in this book is based on the research, opinions, and experiences of the author. It is not intended to replace professional medical advice or treatment. The reader should regularly consult a physician for any health issues and always seek the advice of a physician before modifying diet, supplement, or exercise regimens.

The author and publisher shall have neither liability nor responsibility to any person or entity concerning any loss or damage related to the information contained in this book. The information provided is general in nature and may not apply to every individual. Any reliance on the information contained herein is solely at the reader's own risk.

Contents

Introduction

Chronic kidney disease affects millions of people worldwide, gradually impairing the kidneys' ability to filter waste from the blood. As the disease progresses through several stages, kidney function continues to worsen, eventually leading to complete kidney failure or end-stage renal disease. This necessitates dialysis or a kidney transplant to sustain life.

Coping with chronic kidney disease and renal failure presents many physical, emotional, and lifestyle challenges. From monitoring lab tests to following strict dietary guidelines, patients must make significant adjustments to care for their health. The treatment regimen also includes medications, dialysis sessions, and potential transplant surgery, all of which can impact quality of life.

As a chronic disease, ongoing self-management and patient education are critical. This book aims to provide a comprehensive guide to not just surviving but also thriving with chronic kidney disease. It will explore all aspects of living with renal failure, from understanding the diagnosis to practical home care tips. Topics covered include treatment options, nutrition management, building a support system, and maintaining emotional well-being.

With the right knowledge, adaptations, and a positive attitude, a fulfilling life is possible despite kidney disease. This definitive guide equips patients and their loved ones with the key information needed to effectively manage chronic renal failure and focus on what matters most each day. From treatment decisions to lifestyle adjustments, this handbook covers everything you need to continue enjoying life's moments while on the kidney disease journey.

Chapter 1

Understanding Chronic Kidney Disease

What is Chronic Kidney Disease?

Chronic kidney disease (CKD) is a long-term condition that affects the functioning of the kidneys. The kidneys play a crucial role in filtering waste products and excess fluids from the blood, regulating blood pressure, and producing hormones that stimulate the production of red blood cells. When the kidneys are damaged or unable to function properly, waste products and fluids can build up in the body, leading to various complications.

CKD is a progressive condition, meaning it worsens over time. It is often referred to as a "silent disease" because symptoms may not be noticeable until the kidneys are significantly damaged. The severity of CKD is classified into five stages, with stage 1 being the mildest and stage 5 indicating end-stage renal disease (ESRD), where the kidneys are no longer able to function adequately.

There are several causes and risk factors that can contribute to the development of CKD. The most common causes include high blood pressure and diabetes, which together account for a significant proportion of CKD cases. Other causes include certain autoimmune diseases, genetic disorders, kidney infections, urinary tract obstructions, and prolonged use of certain medications.

High blood pressure, or hypertension, is a leading cause of CKD. When blood pressure is consistently high, it can damage the blood vessels in the kidneys, impairing their ability to filter waste products effectively. Similarly, diabetes, particularly uncontrolled diabetes, can damage the small blood vessels and structures in the kidneys, leading to CKD.

In addition to high blood pressure and diabetes, other risk factors for CKD include obesity, smoking, a family history of kidney disease, older age, and certain ethnic backgrounds, such as African, Hispanic, or Native American descent. It is important to note that having one or more risk factors does not necessarily mean a person will develop CKD, but it does increase the likelihood.

The stages of CKD are determined based on the estimated glomerular filtration rate (eGFR), which measures how well the kidneys are filtering waste from the blood. Stage 1 CKD is characterized by mild kidney damage and a normal or slightly reduced eGFR. As the disease progresses, the eGFR decreases, and symptoms may start to appear. In stage 5 CKD, also known as ESRD, the kidneys have lost nearly all their function, and dialysis or a kidney transplant is necessary to sustain life.

Symptoms of CKD can vary depending on the stage of the disease. In the early stages, there may be no noticeable symptoms. As CKD progresses, common symptoms include fatigue, weakness, loss of appetite, nausea, vomiting, difficulty concentrating, sleep problems, muscle cramps, swelling in the feet and ankles, persistent itching, and changes in urine output (either increased or decreased).

Diagnosing CKD involves a combination of medical history, physical examination, and laboratory tests. Blood tests are used to measure the levels of waste products, such as creatinine and urea, in the blood. Urine tests can detect the presence of protein or blood in the urine, which may indicate kidney damage. Imaging tests, such as ultrasound or CT scans, may be performed to assess the size and structure of the kidneys.

Early detection and management of CKD are crucial in slowing down the progression of the disease and preventing complications. Treatment options for CKD include lifestyle modifications, medication, and, in advanced stages, dialysis or kidney transplantation. Lifestyle modifications may involve following a kidney-friendly diet, maintaining a healthy weight, exercising regularly, managing blood pressure and blood sugar levels, quitting smoking, and limiting alcohol consumption.

Causes and Risk Factors

Chronic kidney disease (CKD) can be caused by a variety of factors, and understanding these causes and risk factors is crucial for managing the condition effectively. In this section, we will explore the common causes of CKD and the factors that increase the risk of developing this condition.

Causes of Chronic Kidney Disease

1. **Diabetes:** Diabetes is the leading cause of CKD. High blood sugar levels can damage kidney blood vessels, impairing filtration. If you have diabetes, it is essential to manage your blood sugar levels carefully to reduce the risk of developing CKD.

2. **High Blood Pressure:** Uncontrolled high blood pressure can also damage the blood vessels in the kidneys, leading to CKD. It is crucial to monitor and manage your blood pressure levels to prevent kidney damage. Lifestyle modifications, such as following a healthy diet and exercising regularly, along with prescribed medications, can help control blood pressure effectively.

3. **Glomerulonephritis:** Glomerulonephritis refers to inflammation of the glomeruli, which are tiny filters in

the kidneys. This condition can be caused by infections, immune system disorders, or certain medications. If left untreated, glomerulonephritis can progress to CKD.

4. **Polycystic Kidney Disease (PKD):** PKD is an inherited condition characterized by the growth of cysts in the kidneys. Gradual replacement of healthy kidney tissue by cysts can lead to Chronic Kidney Disease (CKD). If you have a family history of PKD, it is essential to undergo regular screenings to detect the condition early.

5. **Obstructive Nephropathy:** Obstructive nephropathy occurs when there is a blockage in the urinary tract, preventing the normal flow of urine from the kidneys. This blockage can be caused by conditions such as kidney stones, tumors, or an enlarged prostate gland. If left untreated, obstructive nephropathy can cause kidney damage and eventually lead to CKD.

6. **Recurrent Urinary Tract Infections (UTIs):** Frequent UTIs can increase the risk of developing CKD, especially if the infections spread to the kidneys. It is important to seek prompt treatment for UTIs and take preventive measures, such as maintaining good hygiene and staying hydrated, to reduce the risk of recurrent infections.

7. **Systemic Lupus Erythematosus (SLE):** SLE is an autoimmune disease that can affect various organs, including the kidneys. Inflammation caused by SLE can damage the kidneys and lead to CKD. If you have SLE, it is crucial to work closely with your healthcare team to manage the condition and minimize kidney damage.

Risk Factors for Chronic Kidney Disease

While certain conditions can directly cause CKD, several risk factors can increase the likelihood of developing this condition. These risk factors include:

1. **Age:** The risk of developing CKD increases with age. As we get older, the kidneys may naturally lose some of their function, making them more susceptible to damage.
2. **Family History:** If you have a family history of kidney disease, particularly PKD or other hereditary conditions, your risk of developing CKD is higher. It is important to inform your healthcare provider about your family history so that appropriate screenings can be conducted.
3. **Race and Ethnicity:** Certain racial and ethnic groups, such as African Americans, Hispanics, and Native Americans, have a higher risk of developing CKD. The reasons for these disparities are not yet fully

understood but may be related to genetic factors or higher rates of conditions like diabetes and high blood pressure within these populations.

4. **Obesity:** Being overweight or obese increases the risk of developing CKD. Excess weight puts additional strain on the kidneys and can contribute to the development of conditions like diabetes and high blood pressure, which are major causes of CKD.

5. **Smoking:** Smoking damages blood vessels and reduces blood flow to the kidneys, increasing the risk of kidney damage. Quitting smoking is essential for maintaining kidney health and reducing the risk of CKD.

6. **Certain Medications:** Some medications, such as nonsteroidal anti-inflammatory drugs (NSAIDs) and certain antibiotics, can cause kidney damage if used excessively or for prolonged periods. It is important to use medications as directed and consult with your healthcare provider if you have any concerns.

7. **Exposure to Environmental Toxins:** Long-term exposure to certain environmental toxins, such as heavy metals or chemicals, can damage the kidneys and increase the risk of CKD. It is important to take necessary precautions and follow safety guidelines when working with or around potentially harmful substances.

By understanding the causes and risk factors associated with CKD, you can take proactive steps to prevent or manage the condition effectively. Regular check-ups, maintaining a healthy lifestyle, and working closely with your healthcare team are essential for minimizing the risk of CKD and maintaining optimal kidney health.

Stages of Chronic Kidney Disease

Chronic kidney disease (CKD) is a progressive condition that develops over time. It is important to understand the different stages of CKD to effectively manage the disease and make informed decisions about treatment options. The stages of CKD are determined by the level of kidney function, which is measured by the glomerular filtration rate (GFR). GFR measures kidney function by filtering waste and fluid from blood.

There are five stages of CKD, ranging from mild to severe. Each stage is characterized by specific levels of kidney function and different treatment approaches. It is important to note that CKD is a progressive disease that tends to worsen over time if left untreated. However, with proper management and lifestyle modifications, it is possible to slow down the progression of the disease and maintain a good quality of life.

Stage 1: **Kidney Damage with Normal or High GFR**

In stage 1 of CKD, there is evidence of kidney damage, but the GFR is still normal or high. Kidney damage can be detected through various tests, such as urine tests, blood tests, and imaging studies. Common causes of kidney damage include diabetes, high blood pressure, and certain medications. At this stage, the kidneys are still functioning well, and most people do not experience any symptoms. Treatment focuses on managing the underlying cause of kidney damage and preventing further progression of the disease.

Stage 2: **Mildly Reduced GFR**

In stage 2, there is a mild reduction in GFR, indicating that the kidneys are not functioning at full capacity. The GFR ranges from 60 to 89 mL/min, which is slightly below the normal range. At this stage, some people may start to experience symptoms such as fatigue, mild swelling, and changes in urination patterns. Treatment involves managing symptoms, controlling blood pressure, and making lifestyle modifications to slow down the progression of the disease.

Stage 3: **Moderately Reduced GFR**

Stage 3 is divided into two sub-stages: 3A and 3B, based on the level of GFR. In stage 3A, the GFR ranges from 45 to 59 mL/min, while in stage 3B, the GFR ranges from 30 to 44 mL/min. At this stage, kidney function is significantly reduced, and symptoms become more noticeable. Common symptoms include swelling, fatigue, changes in appetite, and changes in urine output. Treatment focuses on managing symptoms, controlling blood pressure, and making dietary changes to reduce the workload on the kidneys.

Stage 4: **Severely Reduced GFR**

In stage 4, the GFR ranges from 15 to 29 mL/min, indicating a severe reduction in kidney function. At this stage, the kidneys are unable to effectively filter waste and excess fluid from the blood, leading to the buildup of toxins in the body. Symptoms become more severe and may include severe swelling, fatigue, nausea, vomiting, and changes in mental alertness. Treatment options at this stage include dialysis or kidney transplantation, as the kidneys are no longer able to perform their functions adequately.

Stage 5: **End-Stage Kidney Disease**

Stage 5, also known as end-stage kidney disease (ESKD), is the most advanced stage of CKD. The GFR is less than 15 mL/min, indicating that the kidneys have lost almost all of their function. At this stage, the body is unable to maintain a proper balance of fluids and electrolytes, leading to life-threatening complications. Treatment options for ESKD include dialysis or kidney transplantation. Dialysis is a procedure that helps remove waste and excess fluid from the blood, while kidney transplantation involves replacing the failed kidneys with a healthy kidney from a donor.

It is important to note that the progression of CKD can vary from person to person. Some individuals may progress through the stages quickly, while others may progress more slowly. Regular monitoring of kidney function and close collaboration with healthcare professionals are essential for managing CKD effectively and making informed decisions about treatment options.

In the next section, we will explore the symptoms and diagnosis of chronic kidney disease, which can help individuals identify the disease at an early stage and seek appropriate medical care.

Symptoms and Diagnosis

In this section, we will explore the common symptoms of chronic kidney disease (CKD) and the various diagnostic tests used to identify and monitor the condition. It is important to remember that symptoms may vary from person to person, and some individuals may not experience any symptoms at all until the disease has progressed to an advanced stage. However, being aware of the potential signs can help you seek medical attention and receive appropriate treatment on time.

Symptoms of Chronic Kidney Disease

Early stages of CKD often do not present noticeable symptoms. As the disease progresses, however, the following symptoms may manifest:

1. **Fatigue:** Feeling constantly tired and lacking energy is a common symptom of CKD. This can be attributed to the kidneys' reduced ability to produce a hormone called erythropoietin, which stimulates the production of red blood cells.

2. **Swelling:** Also known as edema, swelling can occur in the legs, ankles, feet, and hands. This happens when the kidneys are unable to remove excess fluid and sodium from the body.

3. **Changes in urination:** CKD can cause changes in urination patterns. You may experience increased frequency, especially at night (nocturia), or decreased urine output. Urine may also appear foamy or contain blood.

4. **Persistent itching:** The accumulation of waste products in the blood can lead to persistent itching, often affecting the legs and back.

5. **Shortness of breath:** As CKD progresses, fluid can build up in the lungs, causing difficulty breathing.

6. **High blood pressure:** Kidneys play a crucial role in regulating blood pressure. When they are damaged, blood pressure can rise, leading to hypertension.

7. **Nausea and vomiting:** The buildup of waste products in the blood can cause nausea and vomiting, particularly in the morning.

8. **Loss of appetite:** CKD can affect your sense of taste and cause a loss of appetite, leading to unintended weight loss.

9. **Muscle cramps and twitches:** Electrolyte imbalances, such as low levels of calcium and magnesium, can result in muscle cramps and twitches.

10. **Cognitive difficulties:** In advanced stages of CKD, cognitive function may be impaired, leading to difficulty concentrating, memory problems, and confusion.

It is important to note that these symptoms can also be associated with other health conditions. If you experience any of these symptoms, it is crucial to consult with your healthcare provider for a proper diagnosis.

Diagnosis of Chronic Kidney Disease

To diagnose CKD, healthcare providers utilize a combination of medical history, physical examination, and laboratory tests. The following diagnostic tools are commonly used:

1. **Blood tests:** Blood tests are performed to measure the levels of creatinine, a waste product produced by muscle metabolism, and blood urea nitrogen (BUN), a waste product generated by the breakdown of proteins. Elevated levels of these substances in the blood can indicate impaired kidney function.

2. **Urine tests:** Urine tests, such as a urinalysis, can provide valuable information about kidney function. The presence of protein (albuminuria) or blood in the urine (hematuria) can indicate kidney damage.

3. **Imaging tests:** Imaging tests, such as ultrasound, CT scan, or MRI, may be used to visualize the kidneys and identify any structural abnormalities or blockages.

4. **Kidney biopsy:** In some cases, a kidney biopsy may be necessary to determine the cause and severity of kidney damage. During this procedure, a small sample of kidney tissue is extracted and examined under a microscope.

5. **Glomerular filtration rate (GFR):** GFR is a measure of how well the kidneys are filtering waste products from the blood. It is calculated using a formula that takes into account factors such as age, gender, race, and creatinine levels.

Once a diagnosis of CKD is confirmed, further tests may be conducted to determine the underlying cause and stage of the disease. These additional tests may include imaging studies, genetic testing, and specialized blood tests.

Early detection and diagnosis of CKD are crucial for implementing appropriate treatment strategies and slowing the progression of the disease. Regular monitoring of kidney function through blood and urine tests is essential for individuals with CKD to ensure timely intervention and management.

Remember, if you experience any symptoms or have concerns about your kidney health, it is important to consult with a healthcare professional for an accurate diagnosis and personalized treatment plan.

Chapter 2

Managing Your Diet

The Importance of a Kidney-Friendly Diet

When it comes to managing chronic kidney disease (CKD), one of the most crucial aspects is maintaining a kidney-friendly diet. A well-balanced and nutritious diet can help slow down the progression of the disease, manage symptoms, and improve overall health and well-being. In this section, we will explore the importance of a kidney-friendly diet and provide you with practical tips on how to make healthier food choices.

Understanding the Role of Diet in Kidney Disease

The kidneys play an important role in filtering waste products and excess fluids from the blood. However, when you have CKD, your kidneys are not able to perform this function effectively. As a result, waste products and fluids can build up in your body, leading to various complications. A kidney-friendly diet aims to reduce the workload on the kidneys by controlling the intake of certain nutrients, such as sodium, potassium, phosphorus, and protein.

Controlling Sodium Intake

Sodium, commonly found in table salt and processed foods, can contribute to fluid retention and high blood pressure, both of which can worsen kidney disease. Therefore, it is very important to limit your sodium intake. To achieve this, you can:

- Read food labels and choose low-sodium or sodium-free products.
- Avoid adding salt to your meals while cooking or at the table.
- Opt for fresh or frozen fruits and vegetables instead of canned ones, as they often contain added sodium.
- Use herbs, spices, and other flavorings to enhance the taste of your meals instead of relying on salt.

Managing Potassium Levels

Potassium is a mineral that helps maintain proper heart and muscle function. However, when your kidneys are not functioning well, potassium levels can rise to dangerous levels. To manage potassium intake, consider the following:

- Limit high-potassium foods such as bananas, oranges, tomatoes, potatoes, and avocados.
- Soak high-potassium vegetables in water before cooking to reduce their potassium content.
- Choose low-potassium alternatives, such as apples, berries, cucumbers, and green beans.

- Be cautious with salt substitutes, as they often contain high levels of potassium.

Monitoring Phosphorus Consumption

Phosphorus is a mineral found in many foods, especially those high in protein. When you have CKD, your kidneys may struggle to remove excess phosphorus from your body, leading to imbalances in calcium and phosphorus levels. To control phosphorus intake, consider the following:

- Limit or avoid high-phosphorus foods such as dairy products, nuts, seeds, and processed meats.
- Choose lower-phosphorus alternatives, such as rice milk instead of cow's milk or white bread instead of whole wheat bread.
- Take phosphate binders as prescribed by your healthcare provider to help control phosphorus levels.

Adjusting Protein Intake

Protein is an essential nutrient for building and repairing tissues in the body. However, excessive protein intake can put a strain on the kidneys. Therefore, it is important to strike a balance and adjust your protein intake based on your stage of CKD. Here are some guidelines:

- In the early stages of CKD, a moderate protein intake may be recommended. This typically involves consuming 0.8 grams of protein per kilogram of body weight per day.

- In the later stages of CKD or if you are on dialysis, your protein needs may increase. Your healthcare provider will guide you on the appropriate protein intake for your specific situation.

Hydration and Fluid Control

Proper hydration is essential for overall health, but when you have CKD, you may need to monitor your fluid intake. Too much fluid can strain the kidneys and lead to swelling and high blood pressure. On the other hand, inadequate fluid intake can cause dehydration. Here are some tips for managing fluid intake:

- Follow your healthcare provider's recommendations regarding daily fluid limits.
- Monitor your urine output and body weight to assess your fluid balance.
- Limit your intake of beverages such as soda, coffee, and tea, as they can contribute to fluid overload.
- Choose water as your primary source of hydration and sip it throughout the day.

Seeking Professional Guidance

Managing a kidney-friendly diet can be challenging, especially when you are dealing with CKD. It is crucial to work closely with a registered dietitian who specializes in kidney disease. They can provide personalized guidance, help you create meal plans, and ensure that you are meeting your nutritional needs while managing your kidney disease effectively.

Remember, a kidney-friendly diet is not about deprivation but rather about making healthier choices that support your kidney function and overall well-being. By following the guidelines provided in this section and working with your healthcare team, you can take control of your diet and improve your quality of life with chronic kidney disease.

Understanding Nutritional Requirements

When it comes to managing chronic kidney disease (CKD), understanding your nutritional requirements is crucial. A kidney-friendly diet plays a significant role in slowing down the progression of the disease and maintaining overall health. In this section, we will delve into the specific nutritional requirements for individuals with CKD and provide you with practical tips to help you make informed dietary choices.

The Importance of a Kidney-Friendly Diet

A kidney-friendly diet is designed to reduce the workload on your kidneys and minimize the accumulation of waste products in your body. By following this diet, you can help preserve your kidney function and prevent complications associated with CKD. The key principles of a kidney-friendly diet include:

1. **Limiting Sodium Intake:** Sodium can contribute to fluid retention and high blood pressure, both of which can strain your kidneys. It is essential to reduce your sodium intake by avoiding processed foods, canned soups, and fast food. Instead, opt for fresh, whole foods, and use herbs and spices to add flavor to your meals.

2. **Controlling Protein Consumption:** Protein is an essential nutrient, but excessive intake can put a strain on your kidneys. It is important to strike a balance by consuming an appropriate amount of high-quality protein. Your healthcare provider or dietitian can help determine the right protein intake for you based on your stage of CKD and other individual factors.

3. **Monitoring Phosphorus and Potassium Levels:** As kidney function declines, the ability to regulate phosphorus and potassium levels in the body diminishes. High levels of these minerals can lead to complications such as bone disease and heart problems. To manage these levels, it is crucial to limit foods that are high in phosphorus and potassium, such as dairy products, nuts, and bananas. Your healthcare provider or dietitian can guide you with specific recommendations.

4. **Balancing Fluid Intake:** Individuals with CKD may need to monitor their fluid intake, especially if they experience fluid retention or have reached advanced stages of the disease. Your healthcare provider or dietitian can guide the appropriate amount of fluid you should consume daily.

Understanding Nutritional Requirements

To better understand your nutritional requirements, it is important to consider the stage of CKD you are at. As the disease progresses, your dietary needs may change. Let's explore the nutritional requirements for each stage of CKD:

1. **Stage 1 and 2 CKD:** In the early stages of CKD, your kidneys may still be functioning relatively well. At this stage, your nutritional requirements are similar to those of a healthy individual. It is important to maintain a balanced diet that includes a variety of fruits, vegetables, whole grains, lean proteins, and healthy fats. However, it is advisable to limit sodium intake and avoid excessive consumption of processed foods.

2. **Stage 3 CKD:** As kidney function declines, it becomes necessary to make specific dietary adjustments. Your healthcare provider or dietitian may recommend reducing your protein intake to alleviate the workload on your kidneys. They may also advise limiting phosphorus and potassium-rich foods. It is important to

work closely with your healthcare team to develop a personalized meal plan that meets your nutritional needs.

3. **Stage 4 and 5 CKD:** In the advanced stages of CKD, your kidneys are significantly impaired, and your nutritional requirements may change further. Your healthcare provider or dietitian may recommend further reducing protein intake and closely monitoring phosphorus and potassium levels. In some cases, you may also need to restrict fluid intake. It is crucial to follow their guidance to manage your condition effectively.

Practical Tips for a Kidney-Friendly Diet

Adopting a kidney-friendly diet can seem overwhelming at first, but with the right knowledge and strategies, it can become a manageable part of your daily routine. Here are some practical tips to help you navigate your dietary choices:

1. **Work with a Registered Dietitian:** A registered dietitian who specializes in kidney disease can provide personalized guidance and support. They can help you create a meal plan that meets your nutritional needs while considering your preferences and lifestyle.

2. **Read Food Labels:** When grocery shopping, make it a habit to read food labels carefully. Look for products that are low in sodium, phosphorus, and potassium.

Pay attention to serving sizes to ensure you are consuming an appropriate amount of nutrients.

3. **Cook at Home:** Preparing meals at home gives you more control over the ingredients and allows you to make kidney-friendly substitutions. Experiment with herbs, spices, and low-sodium seasonings to enhance the flavor of your dishes.

4. **Stay Hydrated:** While fluid intake may need to be limited in the advanced stages of CKD, it is still important to stay adequately hydrated. Sip water throughout the day and limit your intake of beverages that are high in sugar or sodium.

5. **Be Mindful of Portion Sizes:** Even with a kidney-friendly diet, portion control is essential. Eating large portions can put additional strain on your kidneys. Use measuring cups or a food scale to ensure you are consuming appropriate serving sizes.

Remember, managing your diet is just one aspect of managing CKD. It is important to work closely with your healthcare team to develop a comprehensive treatment plan that addresses all aspects of your condition. By understanding your nutritional requirements and making informed dietary choices, you can take control of your health and improve your quality of life.

Foods to Include and Avoid

When it comes to managing chronic kidney disease (CKD), your diet plays a crucial role in maintaining your overall health and well-being. Making the right food choices can help slow down the progression of the disease, manage symptoms, and prevent complications. In this section, we will discuss the foods you should include in your diet and the ones you should avoid to support your kidney health.

Including Kidney-Friendly Foods

A kidney-friendly diet focuses on reducing the workload on your kidneys and maintaining a balance of essential nutrients. Here are some foods that you should include in your diet:

1. **High-quality protein:** Protein is an essential nutrient for your body, but it's important to choose the right sources. Opt for high-quality protein sources such as lean meats (chicken, turkey, and fish), eggs, and dairy products. These foods provide essential amino acids without adding excessive strain to your kidneys.

2. **Fruits and vegetables:** Incorporate a variety of fruits and vegetables into your diet. They are rich in vitamins, minerals, and fiber, which are beneficial for your overall health. However, some fruits and vegetables are higher in potassium and phosphorus, so it's important to choose them wisely. Apples, berries, cabbage, cauliflower, and green beans are generally

lower in these minerals and can be included in moderation.

3. **Whole grains:** Whole grains like brown rice, whole wheat bread, and quinoa are excellent sources of fiber and provide essential nutrients. They are a healthier alternative to refined grains and can help regulate blood sugar levels and promote digestive health.

4. **Healthy fats:** Include sources of healthy fats in your diet, such as avocados, olive oil, and nuts. These fats are beneficial for heart health and can help reduce inflammation in your body.

5. **Low-potassium foods:** Potassium is an essential mineral, but too much of it can be harmful to your kidneys. Choose low-potassium foods like apples, berries, cucumbers, and green beans. It's important to work with a registered dietitian to determine the appropriate amount of potassium for your specific needs.

6. **Low-phosphorus foods:** Phosphorus is another mineral that needs to be monitored in your diet. Limit foods that are high in phosphorus, such as dairy products, nuts, and processed foods. Instead, opt for lower-phosphorus alternatives like rice milk, cream cheese, and white bread.

Foods to Avoid or Limit

While there are foods that are beneficial for kidney health, there are also certain foods that you should avoid or limit to prevent further damage to your kidneys. Here are some examples:

1. **High-sodium foods:** Sodium can contribute to high blood pressure and fluid retention, which can put additional strain on your kidneys. Avoid or limit processed foods, canned soups, fast food, and salty snacks. Instead, opt for fresh, homemade meals with minimal added salt.

2. **High-potassium foods:** If your kidneys are not functioning properly, it's important to limit your intake of high-potassium foods. Some examples include bananas, oranges, tomatoes, potatoes, and spinach. These foods can cause potassium levels to rise in your blood, leading to complications. However, it's important to note that potassium requirements may vary depending on the stage of your kidney disease, so consult with your healthcare team or a registered dietitian for personalized guidance.

3. **High-phosphorus foods:** Similar to potassium, high levels of phosphorus in your blood can be harmful to your kidneys. Limit foods that are high in phosphorus, such as dairy products, nuts, seeds, and processed

meats. It's important to read food labels and choose lower-phosphorus alternatives whenever possible.

4. **High-protein foods:** While protein is important, consuming excessive amounts can put strain on your kidneys. Limit your intake of red meat, processed meats, and high-protein dairy products. Instead, choose lean sources of protein and consider incorporating plant-based protein options like legumes and tofu.

5. **Fluid intake:** Depending on the stage of your kidney disease, you may need to monitor your fluid intake. Excessive fluid consumption can lead to fluid retention and strain your kidneys. Your healthcare team will guide the appropriate amount of fluid you should consume daily.

Remember, everyone's dietary needs may vary based on their specific condition and stage of kidney disease. It's important to work closely with a registered dietitian who specializes in kidney disease to create a personalized meal plan that meets your nutritional needs while supporting your kidney health.

In the next section, we will discuss meal planning and provide some kidney-friendly recipes to help you get started on your journey to managing chronic kidney disease through a healthy diet.

Meal Planning and Recipes

When you have chronic kidney disease (CKD), managing your diet becomes crucial to maintaining your overall health and well-being. A kidney-friendly diet can help slow down the progression of the disease, reduce symptoms, and prevent complications. In this section, we will explore the importance of meal planning and provide you with some delicious and nutritious recipes that are suitable for individuals with CKD.

The Importance of Meal Planning

Meal planning is an essential aspect of managing CKD. By carefully selecting and preparing your meals, you can control the intake of certain nutrients that can negatively impact your kidneys. A well-planned diet can help regulate your blood pressure, maintain a healthy weight, and keep your blood sugar levels stable.

One of the key considerations in meal planning for CKD is controlling your intake of sodium, potassium, and phosphorus. These minerals can accumulate in your body when your kidneys are not functioning properly, leading to imbalances and potential complications. By monitoring your intake of these minerals, you can help alleviate the strain on your kidneys and maintain better overall health.

Tips for Meal Planning

Here are some tips to help you with your meal planning:

1. **Consult a Dietitian:** It is highly recommended to consult a registered dietitian who specializes in kidney disease. They can provide personalized guidance and create a meal plan tailored to your specific needs and preferences.

2. **Portion Control:** Pay attention to portion sizes to ensure you are not overeating. This can help you maintain a healthy weight and prevent excessive strain on your kidneys.

3. **Limit Sodium Intake:** Sodium can contribute to fluid retention and high blood pressure. Avoid adding salt to your meals and limit your consumption of processed and packaged foods, which are often high in sodium. Instead, opt for fresh herbs and spices to enhance the flavor of your dishes.

4. **Monitor Potassium and Phosphorus:** Foods rich in potassium and phosphorus, such as bananas, oranges, tomatoes, dairy products, and nuts, should be consumed in moderation. Your dietitian can help you determine the appropriate amount of these minerals for your specific condition.

5. **Choose High-Quality Protein:** Protein is an essential nutrient, but individuals with CKD may need to limit their intake. Choose high-quality protein sources such as lean meats, poultry, fish, and eggs. Plant-based

protein sources like beans, lentils, and tofu are also good options.

6. **Stay Hydrated:** Drinking enough water is important for kidney function. However, if you have fluid restrictions, it is essential to follow your healthcare provider's recommendations. Your dietitian can help you determine the appropriate amount of fluid for your condition.

Kidney-Friendly Recipes

Here are a few kidney-friendly recipes to inspire your meal planning:

1. Grilled Lemon Herb Chicken:

Ingredients:

- 4 boneless, skinless chicken breasts
- 2 tablespoons of lemon juice
- 1 tablespoon of olive oil
- 1 teaspoon dried thyme
- 1 teaspoon dried rosemary
- Salt and pepper to taste

Instructions:

1. In a small bowl, mix lemon juice, olive oil, thyme, rosemary, salt, and pepper.
2. Marinate the chicken breasts in the mixture for at least 30 minutes.

3. Preheat the grill to medium-high heat.
4. Grill the chicken for about 6–8 minutes per side, or until cooked through.
5. Serve with a side of steamed vegetables or a fresh salad.

2. Quinoa and Vegetable Stir-Fry:

Ingredients:
- 1 cup quinoa, cooked according to package instructions
- 1 tablespoon of olive oil
- 1 small onion, diced
- 2 cloves garlic, minced
- 1 cup mixed vegetables (such as bell peppers, carrots, and broccoli)
- 2 tablespoons of low-sodium soy sauce
- 1 tablespoon of rice vinegar
- Salt and pepper to taste

Instructions:
1. Heat olive oil in a large skillet over medium heat.
2. Add the onion and garlic and sauté until fragrant and translucent.
3. Add the mixed vegetables and cook until tender-crisp.
4. Stir in the cooked quinoa, soy sauce, rice vinegar, salt, and pepper.

5. Cook for an additional 2-3 minutes, stirring well to combine.
6. Serve hot as a main dish or a side dish.

3. Berry and Spinach Smoothie:

Ingredients:

- 1 cup fresh or frozen mixed berries (such as strawberries, blueberries, and raspberries)
- 1 cup of fresh spinach leaves
- 1 cup of unsweetened almond milk
- 1 tablespoon honey (optional)

Instructions:

1. Place all the ingredients in a blender and blend until smooth.
2. Add more almond milk if needed to achieve the desired consistency.
3. Taste and add honey if desired for sweetness.
4. Pour into a glass and enjoy it as a refreshing and nutritious snack.

Remember, these recipes are just a starting point. Feel free to modify them according to your taste preferences and dietary restrictions. Experiment with different herbs, spices, and low-sodium seasonings to add flavor to your meals without compromising your kidney health.

By incorporating these meal-planning tips and kidney-friendly recipes into your daily routine, you can take control of your diet and better manage your chronic kidney disease. Remember to consult with your healthcare team and dietitian for personalized advice and guidance.

Chapter 3

Medications and Treatment Options

Common Medications for Chronic Kidney Disease

When it comes to managing chronic kidney disease (CKD), medications play a crucial role in slowing down the progression of the disease and managing its symptoms. In this section, we will explore some of the common medications used in the treatment of CKD.

Blood Pressure Medications

High blood pressure, also known as hypertension, is a common complication of chronic kidney disease. Controlling blood pressure is essential for preserving kidney function and preventing further damage. Several types of medications are commonly prescribed to manage hypertension in individuals with CKD.

1. **Angiotensin-Converting Enzyme (ACE) Inhibitors:** ACE inhibitors work by relaxing blood vessels, reducing the workload on the heart, and lowering blood pressure. They also help to reduce proteinuria, a

condition where excessive amounts of protein are excreted in the urine. Examples of ACE inhibitors include lisinopril, enalapril, and ramipril.

2. **Angiotensin II Receptor Blockers (ARBs):** ARBs are another class of medications that help lower blood pressure and reduce proteinuria. They work by blocking the action of angiotensin II, a hormone that causes blood vessels to narrow. Commonly prescribed ARBs include losartan, valsartan, and irbesartan.

3. **Calcium Channel Blockers:** These medications help relax and widen blood vessels, reducing blood pressure. They also decrease the workload on the heart. Examples of calcium channel blockers include amlodipine, nifedipine, and diltiazem.

4. **Beta-Blockers:** Beta-blockers work by blocking the effects of adrenaline, which helps to lower blood pressure and reduce the workload on the heart. They are often prescribed in combination with other blood pressure medications. Commonly prescribed beta-blockers include metoprolol, carvedilol, and atenolol.

5. **Diuretics:** Diuretics help the body eliminate excess fluid and sodium, reducing blood volume and lowering blood pressure. They are often used in combination with other blood pressure medications. Examples of

diuretics include furosemide, hydrochlorothiazide, and spironolactone.

It is important to note that the choice of blood pressure medication may vary depending on individual factors such as the stage of CKD, the presence of other medical conditions, and any potential drug interactions. Your healthcare provider will determine the most appropriate medication and dosage for you.

Medications for Anemia

Anemia is a common complication of chronic kidney disease, characterized by a decrease in the number of red blood cells or a decrease in their ability to carry oxygen. Anemia can cause fatigue, weakness, and shortness of breath. To manage anemia in individuals with CKD, the following medications are commonly prescribed:

1. **Erythropoiesis-Stimulating Agents (ESAs):** ESAs are synthetic versions of a hormone called erythropoietin, which stimulates the production of red blood cells in the bone marrow. They are administered through injections and help to increase hemoglobin levels and improve the symptoms of anemia. Examples of ESAs include epoetin alfa and darbepoetin alfa.

2. **Iron Supplements:** Iron is essential for the production of red blood cells. In individuals with CKD, iron deficiency is common and can contribute to anemia.

Iron supplements may be prescribed to replenish iron stores and improve red blood cell production. They can be taken orally or administered intravenously.

3. **Vitamin B12 and Folic Acid:** Deficiencies in vitamin B12 and folic acid can also contribute to anemia. Supplements of these vitamins may be prescribed to address deficiencies and improve red blood cell production.

It is important to closely follow your healthcare provider's instructions regarding the use of these medications. Regular monitoring of blood counts and iron levels may be necessary to ensure optimal management of anemia.

Phosphate Binders

Phosphate binders are medications used to control high levels of phosphate in the blood, a common problem in individuals with chronic kidney disease. When the kidneys are not functioning properly, they are unable to effectively remove excess phosphate from the body.

High levels of phosphate can lead to bone and mineral disorders and contribute to the progression of CKD. Phosphate binders work by binding to dietary phosphate in the digestive tract, preventing its absorption into the bloodstream. Some commonly prescribed phosphate binders include calcium carbonate, calcium acetate, and sevelamer.

Medications for Hyperkalemia

Hyperkalemia, or high potassium levels in the blood, is another common complication of chronic kidney disease. It can be dangerous and may cause irregular heart rhythms. Medications called potassium binders may be prescribed to help lower potassium levels. These medications work by binding to potassium in the digestive tract, preventing its absorption into the bloodstream. Examples of potassium binders include sodium polystyrene sulfonate and patiromer.

Other Medications

In addition to the medications mentioned above, individuals with chronic kidney disease may require other medications to manage specific complications or comorbidities. For example:

1. **Statins:** Statins may be prescribed to manage high cholesterol levels, which are common in individuals with CKD.
2. **Anticoagulants:** In some cases, anticoagulant medications may be prescribed to prevent blood clots in individuals with CKD who are at increased risk.
3. **Immunosuppressants:** Individuals who have undergone kidney transplantation may require immunosuppressant medications to prevent rejection of the transplanted kidney.

It is important to work closely with your healthcare provider to ensure that all medications are taken as prescribed and to monitor for any potential side effects or interactions. Regular follow-up appointments and blood tests are essential to assess the effectiveness of the medications and make any necessary adjustments to the treatment plan.

Managing High Blood Pressure

Chronic kidney disease (CKD) can often lead to high blood pressure, also known as hypertension. It's crucial to manage hypertension effectively to slow down the progression of kidney damage and minimize the risk of other complications. In this section, we will discuss the importance of managing high blood pressure, the target blood pressure goals, and various strategies to achieve and maintain healthy blood pressure levels.

The Link Between High Blood Pressure and Kidney Disease

High blood pressure and kidney disease often occur together. Hypertension is one of the major causes of chronic kidney disease (CKD). When blood pressure remains high for a long time, it puts a strain on the blood vessels in the kidneys, which can cause damage over time. This damage can reduce the kidneys' ability to filter waste and excess fluid from the body, leading to a buildup of toxins and fluid retention.

It's important to note that kidney disease can also cause high blood pressure. The kidneys are responsible for regulating blood pressure by maintaining the balance of salt and water in the body. If the kidneys aren't functioning properly, this balance is disrupted, which can result in an increase in blood pressure.

Target Blood Pressure Goals

The target blood pressure goals for individuals with CKD may vary depending on the stage of kidney disease and the presence of other medical conditions. In general, the recommended target blood pressure for most people with CKD is below 130/80 mmHg. However, your healthcare provider may adjust this target based on your specific circumstances.

It is important to note that achieving and maintaining healthy blood pressure levels requires a multifaceted approach that includes lifestyle modifications and, in some cases, medication.

Lifestyle Modifications to Manage High Blood Pressure

1. **Dietary Changes:** A kidney-friendly diet can help manage high blood pressure. This includes reducing sodium intake, limiting processed and packaged foods, and increasing the consumption of fruits, vegetables, whole grains, and lean proteins. Additionally, it is important to monitor potassium and phosphorus levels, as imbalances in these minerals can affect blood pressure.

2. **Weight Management:** Maintaining a healthy weight is crucial for managing high blood pressure. Losing excess weight can significantly lower blood pressure levels. It is recommended to work with a registered dietitian or healthcare provider to develop a personalized weight loss plan that takes into account your specific dietary needs and restrictions.

3. **Regular Physical Activity:** Engaging in regular physical activity can help lower blood pressure and improve overall cardiovascular health. Aim for at least 150 minutes of moderate-intensity aerobic exercise, such as brisk walking or cycling, per week. Consult with your healthcare provider before starting any exercise program, especially if you have other medical conditions.

4. **Stress Management:** Chronic stress can contribute to high blood pressure. Finding healthy ways to manage stress, such as practicing relaxation techniques, engaging in hobbies, or seeking support from a therapist or support group, can help lower blood pressure levels.

5. **Limit Alcohol Consumption:** Excessive alcohol consumption can raise blood pressure levels. It is recommended to limit alcohol intake to moderate levels, which means up to one drink per day for women and up to two drinks per day for men.

6. **Quit Smoking:** Smoking not only increases the risk of kidney disease but also raises blood pressure. Quitting smoking is essential for managing high blood pressure and improving overall health. Seek support from healthcare professionals or support groups to help you quit smoking successfully.

Medications for High Blood Pressure

In some cases, lifestyle modifications alone may not be sufficient to control high blood pressure. Your healthcare provider may prescribe medications to help lower your blood pressure. Some common medications used to manage high blood pressure in individuals with CKD include:

1. **Angiotensin-Converting Enzyme (ACE) Inhibitors:** These medications help relax blood vessels, reducing blood pressure. They also have a protective effect on the kidneys by reducing proteinuria (excessive protein in the urine).

2. **Angiotensin II Receptor Blockers (ARBs):** Similar to ACE inhibitors, ARBs also relax blood vessels and lower blood pressure. They are often prescribed as an alternative to ACE inhibitors for individuals who experience side effects from ACE inhibitors.

3. **Diuretics:** Diuretics help remove excess fluid from the body, reducing blood volume and lowering blood

pressure. They are commonly used in combination with other blood pressure medications.

4. **Calcium Channel Blockers:** These medications relax and widen blood vessels, making it easier for blood to flow and reducing blood pressure.

5. **Beta-Blockers:** Beta-blockers reduce the heart rate and the force of the heart's contractions, thereby lowering blood pressure.

It is important to take medications as prescribed by your healthcare provider and to attend regular follow-up appointments to monitor your blood pressure and adjust the medication regimen if necessary.

Monitoring and Maintaining Healthy Blood Pressure

Regular monitoring of blood pressure is essential for managing high blood pressure effectively. Your healthcare provider may recommend home blood pressure monitoring to track your blood pressure between office visits. This can help identify any fluctuations or trends that may require adjustments to your treatment plan.

Additionally, it is important to maintain regular follow-up appointments with your healthcare provider to monitor your blood pressure, kidney function, and overall health. These appointments provide an opportunity to discuss any concerns or changes in your condition and make necessary adjustments to your treatment plan.

Remember, managing high blood pressure is a lifelong commitment. By adopting a healthy lifestyle, taking prescribed medications, and working closely with your healthcare team, you can effectively manage high blood pressure and reduce the risk of further kidney damage and other complications associated with chronic kidney disease.

Treating Anemia

Anemia is a common complication of chronic kidney disease (CKD) that occurs when your body doesn't have enough healthy red blood cells to carry oxygen to your tissues. It can leave you feeling tired, weak, and short of breath. In this section, we will explore the causes of anemia in CKD and discuss the various treatment options available to manage this condition.

Understanding Anemia in Chronic Kidney Disease

Anemia in CKD is primarily caused by a decrease in the production of erythropoietin (EPO), a hormone produced by the kidneys that stimulates the production of red blood cells in the bone marrow. As kidney function declines, the production of EPO decreases, leading to a decrease in red blood cell production.

Additionally, CKD can cause other factors that contribute to anemia, such as iron deficiency, vitamin deficiencies (particularly vitamin B12 and folate), and inflammation. These factors further impair the body's ability to produce and maintain healthy red blood cells.

Treatment Options for Anemia in Chronic Kidney Disease

The treatment of anemia in CKD aims to increase the production of red blood cells and improve the symptoms associated with anemia. The following are the main treatment options available:

1. Erythropoiesis-Stimulating Agents (ESAs)

ESAs are synthetic forms of erythropoietin that can be prescribed to stimulate the production of red blood cells. They are typically administered through injections or intravenous infusions. ESAs work by mimicking the action of EPO and stimulating the bone marrow to produce more red blood cells.

It is important to note that ESAs should be used judiciously and under the guidance of a healthcare professional. They are not suitable for all patients and may have potential risks and side effects, such as an increased risk of blood clots or high blood pressure. Regular monitoring of hemoglobin levels is necessary to ensure the appropriate dosage of ESAs.

2. Iron Supplementation

Iron plays a crucial role in the production of red blood cells. In CKD, iron deficiency is a common cause of anemia. Iron supplementation can help replenish iron stores and improve red blood cell production. Iron can be administered orally or intravenously, depending on the severity of the deficiency and the patient's response to oral supplementation.

It is important to note that iron supplementation should be closely monitored, as excessive iron levels can be harmful. Regular blood tests are necessary to assess iron levels and adjust the dosage accordingly.

3. Blood Transfusions

In severe cases of anemia, blood transfusions may be necessary to quickly increase the number of red blood cells in the body. Blood transfusions can provide immediate relief from the symptoms of anemia, but they are not a long-term solution. They are typically reserved for emergencies or when other treatment options have failed.

4. Nutritional Support

In some cases, anemia in CKD can be improved by addressing nutritional deficiencies. This may involve dietary changes or the use of oral supplements to ensure an adequate intake of essential nutrients, such as iron, vitamin B12, and folate. A registered dietitian can provide personalized guidance on dietary modifications and recommend appropriate supplements.

Dialysis and Transplantation

Dialysis and transplantation are two treatment options for individuals with chronic kidney disease (CKD) who have reached the advanced stages of the condition. These interventions are designed to help manage the symptoms of CKD and improve overall quality of life. In this section, we will explore the different types of dialysis, the process of transplantation, and what to expect from these treatments.

Dialysis

Dialysis is a medical procedure that removes waste products and excess fluid from the blood when the kidneys are unable to perform this function. There are two main types of dialysis: hemodialysis and peritoneal dialysis.

1. **Hemodialysis:** Hemodialysis is the most commonly used form of dialysis and is usually conducted in a hospital or dialysis center. The process involves using a dialyzer machine to filter the blood. The patient's blood is passed through the dialyzer where it gets rid of excess fluids and waste products before being returned to the body.

   Hemodialysis treatments usually last around four hours and are typically performed three times a week. The frequency and duration of treatments may vary depending on the individual's specific needs and the recommendations of their healthcare team.

2. **Peritoneal Dialysis:** Peritoneal dialysis is a type of dialysis that can be done at home. This method uses the peritoneum, which is the lining of the abdomen, as a natural filter. A catheter is surgically placed in the abdomen, and a special dialysis solution is introduced into the peritoneal cavity. The solution soaks up waste products and excess fluid from the blood, which is then removed from the body.

   Peritoneal dialysis offers more flexibility and independence compared to hemodialysis. It can be performed during the day or night, allowing individuals to continue with their daily activities while receiving treatment. However, it requires regular exchanges of the dialysis solution and careful adherence to hygiene practices to prevent infections.

Transplantation

Kidney transplantation is considered the best treatment option for individuals with end-stage renal disease (ESRD) who are suitable candidates. A kidney transplant involves surgically placing a healthy kidney from a living or deceased donor into the recipient's body. This new kidney takes over the function of the failed kidneys, allowing the individual to regain kidney function and eliminate the need for dialysis.

1. **Finding a Donor:** Finding a suitable kidney donor can be a challenging process. There are two main types of kidney donors: living donors and deceased donors.

   Living donors are usually family members or close friends who are willing to donate one of their kidneys. In some cases, individuals may also choose to donate a kidney altruistically to a stranger. Living-donor transplants have a higher success rate and offer the advantage of being able to schedule the transplant in advance.

   Deceased donors are individuals who have registered as organ donors or whose families have consented to organ donation after their passing. The availability of deceased donor kidneys depends on the number of organs available for transplantation and the compatibility between the donor and recipient.

2. **The Transplant Process:** The kidney transplant process involves several steps, including evaluation, matching, surgery, and post-transplant care.

   - **Evaluation:** Before a transplant can take place, both the recipient and potential living donors undergo a thorough evaluation to assess their overall health and compatibility. This evaluation includes blood tests, imaging studies, and consultations with various healthcare professionals.

- **Matching:** For a successful transplant, the donor kidney must be a close match to the recipient's blood and tissue type. This helps reduce the risk of rejection and improves the chances of long-term success. The matching process is done through a national organ transplant waiting list or paired exchange programs.

- **Surgery:** The transplant surgery is performed under general anesthesia. The surgeon places the new kidney in the lower abdomen and connects it to the recipient's blood vessels and bladder. The procedure usually takes a few hours, and the recipient will be closely monitored in the hospital for several days afterward.

- **Post-transplant care:** After the transplant, the recipient will need to take immunosuppressant medications to prevent rejection of the new kidney. Regular follow-up appointments and monitoring will be necessary to ensure the kidney is functioning properly and to address any potential complications.

Considerations and Outlook

Both dialysis and transplantation have their advantages and disadvantages. Dialysis provides a life-sustaining treatment option for individuals who are not suitable candidates for transplantation or are awaiting a suitable donor. It helps manage the symptoms of CKD and allows individuals to maintain a relatively normal lifestyle. However, it requires regular visits to a dialysis center or performing treatments at home.

Transplantation offers the best long-term outcomes for individuals with ESRD. It provides the opportunity for improved quality of life, freedom from dialysis, and the potential for a longer lifespan. However, the availability of suitable donors and the need for lifelong immunosuppressant medications are important factors to consider.

Individuals with CKD need to discuss their treatment options with their healthcare team and make an informed decision based on their specific circumstances. Each person's journey with kidney disease is unique, and the choice between dialysis and transplantation should be made in collaboration with healthcare professionals, taking into account individual preferences, medical history, and available resources.

Alternative and Complementary Therapies

When it comes to managing chronic kidney disease (CKD), traditional medical treatments such as medications, dialysis, and transplantation are often the primary focus. However, many individuals with CKD also explore alternative and complementary therapies to help support their overall well-being and potentially improve their kidney function.

These therapies can be used alongside conventional treatments and may provide additional benefits. In this section, we will explore some of the alternative and complementary therapies that individuals with CKD may consider.

1. **Acupuncture:** Acupuncture is an ancient Chinese practice that involves the insertion of thin needles into specific points on the body. It is believed to help restore the flow of energy, known as Qi, throughout the body. Some studies have suggested that acupuncture may help improve kidney function and reduce symptoms associated with CKD, such as fatigue and pain. However, more research is needed to fully understand the effectiveness of acupuncture in treating CKD.

2. **Herbal Remedies:** Herbal remedies have been used for centuries in various cultures to treat a wide range of health conditions, including kidney disease. Some herbs, such as dandelion root, nettle leaf, and

astragalus, are believed to have diuretic properties and may help support kidney function. However, it is important to note that herbal remedies can interact with medications and may not be suitable for everyone. It is crucial to consult with a healthcare professional before incorporating any herbal remedies into your treatment plan.

3. **Dietary Supplements:** Certain dietary supplements, such as omega-3 fatty acids, coenzyme Q10, and vitamin D, have been studied for their potential benefits in individuals with CKD. Omega-3 fatty acids, found in fish oil, may help reduce inflammation and improve cardiovascular health, which is often a concern for individuals with CKD. Coenzyme Q10 is an antioxidant that may help protect the kidneys from damage. Vitamin D plays a crucial role in bone health and may be beneficial for individuals with CKD who are at risk of developing bone and mineral disorders. However, it is important to discuss the use of dietary supplements with your healthcare provider, as they can interact with medications and may have side effects.

4. **Mind-Body Therapies:** Stress management is an essential aspect of managing CKD, as stress can negatively impact overall health and well-being. Mind-body therapies, such as meditation, yoga, and tai chi, can help reduce stress and promote relaxation.

These practices have also been shown to improve sleep quality, reduce anxiety and depression, and enhance overall quality of life. Incorporating mind-body therapies into your daily routine can be a valuable addition to your CKD management plan.

5. **Massage Therapy:** Massage therapy involves the manipulation of soft tissues in the body to promote relaxation and relieve muscle tension. It can be particularly beneficial for individuals with CKD who experience muscle cramps and pain. Massage therapy may also help improve circulation and reduce stress. However, it is important to choose a qualified and experienced massage therapist who is knowledgeable about CKD and its potential complications.

6. **Exercise and Physical Activity:** Regular exercise and physical activity are crucial for maintaining overall health and well-being, especially for individuals with CKD. Engaging in low-impact exercises, such as walking, swimming, and cycling, can help improve cardiovascular health, strengthen muscles, and enhance flexibility. Exercise can also help manage weight, reduce stress, and improve mood. However, it is important to consult with your healthcare provider before starting any exercise program, as certain activities may need to be modified based on your individual needs and limitations.

7. **Chiropractic Care:** Chiropractic care focuses on the diagnosis and treatment of musculoskeletal disorders, particularly those affecting the spine. Some individuals with CKD may experience back pain or other musculoskeletal issues, which can be addressed through chiropractic adjustments. Chiropractic care may help alleviate pain, improve mobility, and enhance overall well-being. However, it is important to choose a qualified and licensed chiropractor who is familiar with CKD and its potential complications.

8. **Energy Healing:** Energy healing practices, such as Reiki and therapeutic touch, involve the manipulation of energy fields to promote healing and balance within the body. These practices are based on the belief that imbalances in energy can contribute to illness and disease. While there is limited scientific evidence to support the effectiveness of energy healing in treating CKD, some individuals find these therapies to be beneficial in reducing stress, promoting relaxation, and improving overall well-being.

It is important to note that alternative and complementary therapies should not replace conventional medical treatments for CKD. These therapies should be used as adjunctive treatments to support overall health and swell-being. It is crucial to consult with your healthcare provider before incorporating any alternative or complementary therapies into your treatment plan, as they may interact with medications or have potential side effects.

Your healthcare provider can help guide you in making informed decisions about which therapies that may be appropriate for you and how to safely incorporate them into your CKD management plan.

Managing Medications and Treatment Side Effects

When it comes to managing chronic kidney disease (CKD), medications and treatment play a crucial role. However, it's important to be aware that, along with the benefits, medications can also come with potential side effects. In this section, we will explore how to effectively manage medications and navigate any treatment side effects that may arise.

Understanding Medications for CKD

There are various medications that your healthcare provider may prescribe to help manage your CKD. These medications can serve different purposes, such as controlling blood pressure, treating anemia, or reducing inflammation. It's essential to understand the purpose of each medication and how it can benefit your overall kidney health.

Communicating with Your Healthcare Provider

Open and honest communication with your healthcare provider is key to effectively managing your medications and treatment side effects. Make sure to inform them about any existing medical conditions, allergies, or medications you are currently taking. This will help them make informed decisions and avoid any potential drug interactions or adverse reactions.

Additionally, don't hesitate to ask questions or seek clarification about your medications. Understanding why you are taking a particular medication, how it works, and what potential side effects to watch out for can empower you to take an active role in your treatment.

Adhering to the Medication Schedule

Consistency is crucial when it comes to taking medications for CKD. It's important to follow the prescribed dosage and schedule provided by your healthcare provider. Set reminders or use pill organizers to help you stay on track.

If you find it challenging to remember to take your medications, consider incorporating them into your daily routine. For example, you could take them with meals or at the same time each day. If you experience difficulties swallowing pills, discuss alternative options such as liquid formulations or smaller pill sizes with your healthcare provider.

Managing Medication Side Effects

While medications can be beneficial, they can also come with side effects. It's important to be aware of potential side effects and know how to manage them effectively. Here are some common side effects and strategies to address them:

1. **Nausea and Upset Stomach:** If you experience nausea or an upset stomach after taking your medications, try taking them with food. If the symptoms persist, inform your healthcare provider, as they may be able to adjust the dosage or prescribe an alternative medication.

2. **Fatigue and Drowsiness:** Some medications can cause fatigue or drowsiness. If you find that your energy levels are significantly affected, discuss this with your healthcare provider. They may be able to adjust the dosage or recommend alternative medications that have fewer sedative effects.

3. **Dry Mouth:** Certain medications can cause dry mouth. Staying hydrated by drinking plenty of water throughout the day can help alleviate this symptom. You can also try sugar-free gum or lozenges to stimulate saliva production.

4. **Skin Rash or Allergic Reactions:** If you develop a skin rash or experience any signs of an allergic reaction, such as itching or swelling, seek medical attention immediately. These symptoms could indicate

an adverse reaction to the medication and should not be ignored.

5. **Changes in Urination:** Some medications can affect urine output or color. If you notice any significant changes in your urine, such as increased frequency, decreased volume, or unusual color, inform your healthcare provider.

Remember, everyone's response to medications can vary, and not everyone will experience side effects. However, it's important to be vigilant and report any unusual symptoms to your healthcare provider promptly.

Monitoring and Reporting

Regular monitoring of your kidney function and overall health is essential. Your healthcare provider may order blood tests to assess your kidney function, electrolyte levels, and other important markers. These tests help determine the effectiveness of your medications and identify any potential issues.

If you notice any changes in your symptoms or experience new symptoms, it's crucial to report them to your healthcare provider. They can evaluate whether any adjustments to your medications or treatment plan are necessary.

Seeking Support

Managing medications and treatment side effects can be challenging, both physically and emotionally. It's important to seek support from your healthcare team, family, and friends. They can provide guidance and encouragement and help you navigate any difficulties you may encounter.

Additionally, support groups or online communities can be valuable resources for connecting with others who are going through similar experiences. Sharing your concerns, experiences, and tips with others can provide a sense of camaraderie and help you feel less alone in your journey.

Remember, managing medications and treatment side effects is an ongoing process. By staying informed, communicating with your healthcare provider, and seeking support, you can effectively manage your CKD and improve your overall quality of life.

Chapter 4

Lifestyle Modifications

Exercise and Physical Activity

Exercise and physical activity play a crucial role in managing chronic kidney disease (CKD). While it may seem counterintuitive to engage in physical activity when you're dealing with a chronic illness, regular exercise can have numerous benefits for your overall health and well-being. In this section, we will explore the importance of exercise for individuals with CKD and provide practical tips on how to incorporate physical activity into your daily routine.

The Benefits of Exercise for CKD

Regular exercise offers a wide range of benefits for individuals with CKD. Here are some of the key advantages:

1. **Improved cardiovascular health:** Engaging in physical activity helps strengthen your heart and improve blood circulation. This can reduce the risk of cardiovascular complications, such as heart disease and stroke, which are common in individuals with CKD.

2. **Better blood pressure control:** High blood pressure is a common complication of CKD. Regular exercise can help lower blood pressure levels, reducing the strain on your kidneys and protecting them from further damage.

3. **Weight management:** Maintaining a healthy weight is essential for managing CKD. Exercise can help you achieve and maintain a healthy weight by burning calories and building muscle mass.

4. **Enhanced mood and mental health:** Dealing with a chronic illness like CKD can take a toll on your mental well-being. Exercise releases endorphins, which are natural mood boosters, and can help reduce symptoms of anxiety and depression.

5. **Increased energy levels:** Fatigue is a common symptom of CKD. Engaging in regular physical activity can help improve your energy levels and combat fatigue, allowing you to perform daily activities more easily.

6. **Improved bone health:** CKD can lead to bone and mineral disorders, such as osteoporosis. Weight-bearing exercises, such as walking or strength training, can help improve bone density and reduce the risk of fractures.

Safe and Effective Exercise for CKD

Before starting any exercise program, it is important to consult with your healthcare team, including your nephrologist and a qualified exercise professional. They can provide personalized recommendations based on your specific health condition and fitness level. Here are some general guidelines to keep in mind:

1. **Start slowly:** If you have been inactive or have not exercised in a while, it is important to start slowly and gradually increase the intensity and duration of your workouts. This will help prevent injury and allow your body to adapt to the increased physical activity.

2. **Choose low-impact activities:** Low-impact exercises are gentle on the joints and reduce the risk of injury. Examples include walking, swimming, cycling, and using an elliptical machine. Avoid high-impact activities that put excessive stress on your joints, such as running or jumping.

3. **Include a variety of exercises:** Incorporate a mix of cardiovascular exercises, strength training, and flexibility exercises into your routine. Cardiovascular exercises, such as brisk walking or swimming, help improve heart health. Strength training exercises, using light weights or resistance bands, can help build muscle mass. Flexibility exercises, such as stretching

or yoga, improve joint mobility and reduce the risk of injury.

4. **Listen to your body:** Pay attention to how your body feels during and after exercise. If you experience pain, dizziness, or shortness of breath, stop exercising and consult with your healthcare team. It is important to find the right balance between challenging yourself and not overexerting your body.

5. **Stay hydrated:** Drink plenty of water before, during, and after exercise to stay hydrated. Dehydration can put additional strain on your kidneys, so it is important to maintain adequate fluid intake.

6. **Monitor your vital signs:** If you have any cardiovascular complications, such as high blood pressure or heart disease, it may be beneficial to monitor your heart rate and blood pressure during exercise. Your healthcare team can provide guidance on target heart rate zones and safe blood pressure ranges.

7. **Be consistent:** Aim for at least 150 minutes of moderate-intensity aerobic exercise or 75 minutes of vigorous-intensity aerobic exercise per week, spread out over several days. Additionally, incorporate strength training exercises at least two days a week. Consistency is key to reaping the benefits of exercise.

Overcoming Barriers to Exercise

While exercise is beneficial for individuals with CKD, it is not always easy to incorporate physical activity into your daily routine. Here are some common barriers to exercise and strategies to overcome them:

1. **Fatigue:** If you experience fatigue, try breaking your exercise sessions into shorter, more manageable periods throughout the day. Gradually increase the duration and intensity as your energy levels improve.

2. **Time constraints:** If you have a busy schedule, try to find pockets of time for physical activity. This could include taking short walks during your lunch break, using stairs instead of elevators, or incorporating exercise into your daily chores.

3. **Lack of motivation:** Find an exercise buddy or join a support group to stay motivated. Having someone to exercise with can make the experience more enjoyable and help you stay accountable.

4. **Physical limitations:** If you have physical limitations or mobility issues, work with a qualified exercise professional who can design a personalized exercise program that suits your needs and abilities.

Remember, any amount of physical activity is better than none. Even small changes, such as taking short walks or stretching regularly, can have a positive impact on your health.

In the next section, we will explore the importance of managing stress and mental health when living with chronic kidney disease.

Managing Stress and Mental Health

Living with chronic kidney disease (CKD) can be a challenging and stressful experience. Not only do you have to manage the physical symptoms and treatment of the disease, but you also need to take care of your mental and emotional well-being.

Stress and mental health play a crucial role in managing CKD, as they can impact your overall health and quality of life. In this section, we will explore various strategies and techniques to help you effectively manage stress and maintain good mental health while living with CKD.

The Impact of Stress on CKD

Stress is a natural response to challenging situations, and it affects everyone differently. However, for individuals with CKD, stress can have a more significant impact on their health. When you experience stress, your body releases stress hormones like cortisol, which can increase blood pressure and heart rate. These physiological responses can be particularly harmful to individuals with CKD, as they already have compromised kidney function.

Moreover, stress can also lead to unhealthy coping mechanisms such as overeating, smoking, or excessive alcohol consumption, which can further worsen kidney function and overall health. Additionally, stress can negatively affect your mental health, leading to anxiety, depression, and a decreased quality of life. Therefore, it is crucial to develop effective strategies to manage stress and promote mental well-being.

Stress Management Techniques

1. **Identify and Address Stressors:** The first step in managing stress is to identify the factors that contribute to your stress levels. It could be work-related, financial concerns, relationship issues, or even the challenges of managing CKD itself. Once you identify the stressors, try to find ways to address them. This may involve seeking support from loved ones, seeking professional help, or making necessary lifestyle changes.

2. **Practice Relaxation Techniques:** It's important to take steps to reduce stress in your daily life. Relaxation techniques, such as deep breathing exercises, meditation, yoga, and progressive muscle relaxation, can be helpful in promoting a sense of calm. Try experimenting with different techniques until you find one that works for you, and then make it a part of your daily routine.

3. **Exercise Regularly:** Regular physical activity is not only crucial for maintaining good health, but it can also help in managing stress levels. Engaging in moderate-intensity exercise for at least 30 minutes most days of the week triggers the release of endorphins, which are natural mood boosters. Consult with your healthcare team to determine the most suitable exercise regimen for your condition.

4. **Maintain a Healthy Lifestyle:** A healthy lifestyle can significantly impact your stress levels and mental well-being. Ensure you are getting enough sleep, eating a balanced diet, and avoiding excessive caffeine and alcohol consumption. These lifestyle factors can help regulate your mood and energy levels.

5. **Seek Support:** Living with CKD can be emotionally challenging, and it is essential to have a support system in place. Reach out to family, friends, or support groups who can provide understanding, empathy, and encouragement. Consider joining a CKD support group where you can connect with others who are going through similar experiences.

6. **Practice Self-Care:** Taking care of yourself is crucial for managing stress and maintaining good mental health. Engage in activities that bring you joy and relaxation, such as reading, listening to music, spending time in nature, or pursuing hobbies. Prioritize

self-care and make time for activities that nourish your mind, body, and soul.

7. **Manage Time and Prioritize Tasks:** Feeling overwhelmed and stressed can often be a result of poor time management and an overloaded schedule. Learn to prioritize tasks, delegate responsibilities when possible, and set realistic goals. Breaking tasks into smaller, manageable steps can also help reduce stress and increase productivity.

8. **Consider Therapy or Counseling:** If you notice that stress and mental health problems are significantly affecting your day-to-day life, it might be a good idea to seek professional help. Therapy or counseling can offer you the necessary tools and assistance to manage stress, deal with your emotions, and enhance your overall well-being. Remember to prioritize your mental health and seek help when needed.

Remember, managing stress and mental health is an ongoing process. It may take time to find the strategies that work best for you. Be patient with yourself and be open to trying different techniques until you find what resonates with you. By prioritizing your mental well-being and effectively managing stress, you can improve your overall quality of life while living with CKD.

Quitting Smoking and Limiting Alcohol

When it comes to managing chronic kidney disease (CKD), making lifestyle modifications is crucial. Two important changes you can make to improve your kidney health are quitting smoking and limiting alcohol consumption. In this section, we will explore the impact of smoking and alcohol on kidney function and provide practical tips to help you quit smoking and reduce your alcohol intake.

The Impact of Smoking on Kidney Function

Smoking is a harmful habit that affects almost every organ in your body, including your kidneys. Research has shown that smoking can accelerate the progression of CKD and increase the risk of developing kidney failure. Smoking damages blood vessels and reduces blood flow to the kidneys, impairing their ability to filter waste products effectively. This can lead to a buildup of toxins in the body and further damage to the kidneys.

In addition to its direct impact on kidney function, smoking also increases the risk of developing other conditions that can worsen CKD, such as high blood pressure and cardiovascular disease. It is important to note that secondhand smoke can also be harmful, so if you live with a smoker, it is essential to minimize your exposure.

Tips for Quitting Smoking

Quitting smoking is not easy, but it is one of the best things you can do for your overall health, including your kidneys. Here are some tips to help you kick the habit:

1. **Set a quit date:** Choose a specific date to quit smoking and mark it on your calendar. This will give you a clear goal to work toward.

2. **Seek support:** Inform your family, friends, and healthcare team about your decision to quit smoking. Their support and encouragement can make a significant difference in your journey.

3. **Find alternatives:** Replace smoking with healthier habits such as chewing sugar-free gum, snacking on fruits or vegetables, or engaging in physical activity whenever you feel the urge to smoke.

4. **Consider nicotine replacement therapy:** Nicotine replacement products like patches, gum and lozenges can help with withdrawal symptoms and cravings. Consult your healthcare provider to determine the best option for you.

5. **Join a support group:** Connecting with others who are also trying to quit smoking can provide valuable support and motivation. Look for local support groups or online communities where you can share your experiences and learn from others.

6. **Stay positive:** Quitting smoking is a journey, and setbacks may happen. If you slip up and have a cigarette, don't be too hard on yourself. Learn from the experience and recommit to your goal of quitting.

Remember, quitting smoking is a process, and it may take several attempts before you succeed. Stay persistent and focused on your goal, and celebrate each milestone along the way.

The Impact of Alcohol on Kidney Function

While moderate alcohol consumption may not pose significant risks to individuals with healthy kidneys, excessive or chronic alcohol use can have detrimental effects on kidney function. Alcohol is a diuretic, meaning it increases urine production and can lead to dehydration. Dehydration puts strain on the kidneys and can impair their ability to filter waste products effectively.

Moreover, excessive alcohol consumption can lead to high blood pressure, a major risk factor for CKD. Alcohol also interferes with the body's ability to regulate electrolyte levels, which can disrupt kidney function. Additionally, heavy drinking can contribute to liver disease, which can further impact kidney health.

Tips for Limiting Alcohol Consumption

If you have CKD, it is important to limit your alcohol intake to protect your kidneys. Here are some practical tips to help you reduce your alcohol consumption:

1. **Set limits:** Determine how many days a week you will consume alcohol and set a maximum number of drinks per occasion. Stick to these limits and track your alcohol intake to ensure you stay within them.

2. **Choose non-alcoholic alternatives:** When socializing or attending events where alcohol is served, opt for non-alcoholic beverages such as water, herbal tea, or mocktails. This will help you avoid the temptation to drink excessively.

3. **Find healthier coping mechanisms:** If you tend to turn to alcohol as a way to cope with stress or negative emotions, explore alternative strategies such as exercise, meditation, or talking to a trusted friend or therapist.

4. **Seek support:** If you find it challenging to limit your alcohol consumption on your own, consider joining a support group or seeking professional help. There are resources available to assist you in overcoming alcohol dependence.

5. **Be mindful of hidden alcohol:** Some medications, mouthwashes, and cooking ingredients contain alcohol. Read labels carefully and consult your healthcare

provider or pharmacist to ensure you are aware of any hidden sources of alcohol in your daily life.

Remember, moderation is key. If you choose to consume alcohol, do so in moderation, and always consult with your healthcare provider to determine what is safe and appropriate for your specific condition.

By quitting smoking and limiting alcohol consumption, you are taking proactive steps to protect your kidney health and improve your overall well-being. These lifestyle modifications, combined with a kidney-friendly diet and appropriate medical treatment, can significantly slow down the progression of CKD and enhance your quality of life. Stay committed to your goals and seek support when needed. You have the power to make positive changes and thrive despite kidney disease.

Maintaining a Healthy Weight

Maintaining a healthy weight is crucial for individuals with chronic kidney disease (CKD). Excess weight can put additional strain on the kidneys and worsen the progression of the disease. On the other hand, being underweight can lead to malnutrition and weaken the body's ability to fight infections. Therefore, finding and maintaining a healthy weight is essential for managing CKD and improving overall health.

The Impact of Weight on Kidney Health

Carrying excess weight can have a significant impact on kidney health. When you are overweight, your kidneys have to work harder to filter waste products and toxins from the body. This increased workload can lead to further damage to the kidneys and accelerate the progression of CKD.

Additionally, obesity is often associated with other health conditions such as high blood pressure and diabetes, which are major risk factors for kidney disease. By maintaining a healthy weight, you can reduce the risk of developing these conditions and potentially slow down the progression of CKD.

Setting Realistic Weight Goals

When it comes to weight management, it is important to set realistic goals that are achievable and sustainable. Rapid weight loss or extreme dieting can be harmful to individuals with CKD, as it may lead to muscle wasting and nutrient deficiencies. Instead, focus on making gradual and long-term lifestyle changes that promote a healthy weight.

Consulting with a registered dietitian who specializes in kidney disease can be immensely helpful in developing a personalized weight management plan. They can assess your current weight, body composition, and nutritional needs to create a plan that suits your specific circumstances.

Healthy Eating for Weight Management

A kidney-friendly diet is not only beneficial for managing CKD but also for maintaining a healthy weight. Here are some dietary guidelines to support weight management:

1. **Portion Control:** It is important to be mindful of portion sizes and avoid overeating. One effective way to control portion sizes is by using smaller plates and bowls, which can help visually cue appropriate portions.

2. **Balanced Meals:** Make sure to include a variety of nutrient-dense foods in your meals, such as fruits, vegetables, whole grains, lean proteins, and healthy fats, which provide essential nutrients and keep you satisfied.

3. **Limit Sodium Intake:** Excessive sodium consumption can lead to fluid retention and high blood pressure. Choose low-sodium alternatives and avoid processed and packaged foods that are typically high in sodium.

4. **Watch Your Fluid Intake:** While it is important to stay hydrated, individuals with CKD may need to limit their fluid intake. Excessive fluid consumption can lead to fluid overload and strain the kidneys. Consult with your healthcare team to determine the appropriate fluid restriction for your condition.

5. **Limit Added Sugars and Unhealthy Fats:** Foods high in added sugars and unhealthy fats can contribute

to weight gain and increase the risk of developing other health conditions. Opt for natural sugars found in fruits and limit the consumption of sugary beverages, desserts, and processed snacks.

Physical Activity and Weight Management

In addition to a healthy diet, regular physical activity is crucial for maintaining a healthy weight and managing CKD. Exercise offers numerous benefits, including:

1. **Weight Loss:** Engaging in regular physical activity can help burn calories and promote weight loss. Aim for at least 150 minutes of moderate-intensity aerobic exercise, such as brisk walking or cycling, per week.

2. **Improved Cardiovascular Health:** Exercise helps strengthen the heart and improve cardiovascular health, reducing the risk of heart disease, a common complication of CKD.

3. **Increased Muscle Strength:** Resistance training exercises, such as lifting weights or using resistance bands, can help build muscle strength and improve overall body composition.

4. **Enhanced Mental Well-Being:** Physical activity releases endorphins, which can improve mood and reduce stress and anxiety.

Before starting any exercise program, it is important to consult with your healthcare team. They can guide the types and intensity of exercises that are safe and appropriate for your condition.

Monitoring Progress and Seeking Support

Monitoring your weight regularly can help you track your progress and make necessary adjustments to your weight management plan. However, it is important to remember that weight is not the only indicator of health. Focus on overall well-being, including improvements in energy levels, blood pressure, and blood sugar control.

Seeking support from healthcare professionals, support groups, or loved ones can also be beneficial. They can provide encouragement, accountability, and guidance throughout your weight management journey.

Remember, maintaining a healthy weight is a lifelong commitment. By making gradual and sustainable changes to your diet and lifestyle, you can not only manage your weight but also improve your overall health and well-being while living with chronic kidney disease.

Chapter 5

Managing Complications

Cardiovascular Health and Kidney Disease

Cardiovascular health is a crucial aspect of managing chronic kidney disease (CKD). People with CKD are at a higher risk of developing cardiovascular complications, such as heart disease and stroke. Cardiovascular disease is the leading cause of death among individuals with CKD. Therefore, it is essential to prioritize cardiovascular health when managing kidney disease.

Understanding the Connection

The link between cardiovascular health and kidney disease is bidirectional. CKD can contribute to the development of cardiovascular disease, and cardiovascular disease can worsen kidney function.

The kidneys play a vital role in maintaining a healthy cardiovascular system by regulating blood pressure, removing waste products, and balancing electrolytes. When the kidneys are damaged, these functions are compromised, leading to an increased risk of cardiovascular problems.

Hypertension and Kidney Disease

High blood pressure, also known as hypertension, is a common complication of kidney disease. Hypertension is both a cause and a consequence of CKD. When the kidneys are not functioning properly, they struggle to regulate blood pressure effectively. As a result, blood pressure can rise, leading to further damage to the kidneys and an increased risk of cardiovascular events.

Managing hypertension is crucial for individuals with kidney disease. Lifestyle modifications, such as adopting a kidney-friendly diet, reducing sodium intake, and engaging in regular physical activity, can help control blood pressure. Additionally, medications, such as angiotensin-converting enzyme (ACE) inhibitors or angiotensin receptor blockers (ARBs), may be prescribed to manage hypertension and protect kidney function.

Heart Disease and Kidney Disease

Heart disease is a significant concern for individuals with CKD. The presence of kidney disease increases the risk of developing various cardiovascular conditions, including coronary artery disease, heart failure, and arrhythmias. The relationship between kidney disease and heart disease is complex and multifactorial.

One of the primary reasons for the increased risk of heart disease in CKD is the presence of traditional risk factors such as hypertension, diabetes, and high cholesterol. These risk factors are more prevalent in individuals with kidney disease and contribute to the development of cardiovascular complications. Additionally, the presence of inflammation, oxidative stress, and mineral and bone disorders in CKD can further contribute to heart disease.

Managing Cardiovascular Health

To effectively manage cardiovascular health in the context of kidney disease, a comprehensive approach is necessary. Here are some key strategies:

1. **Blood Pressure Control:** Maintaining optimal blood pressure is crucial for individuals with CKD. Regular monitoring of blood pressure levels and adherence to prescribed medications are essential. Lifestyle modifications, such as reducing sodium intake, engaging in regular physical activity, and managing stress, can also help control blood pressure.

2. **Cholesterol Management:** High cholesterol levels are a risk factor for cardiovascular disease. Individuals with CKD should work with their healthcare team to manage cholesterol levels through lifestyle modifications and, if necessary, medication.

3. **Diabetes Management:** Diabetes and kidney disease often coexist. Proper management of diabetes is essential to prevent further kidney damage and reduce

the risk of cardiovascular complications. This includes monitoring blood sugar levels, adhering to a diabetic diet, taking prescribed medications, and engaging in regular physical activity.

4. **Smoking Cessation:** Smoking is a significant risk factor for both kidney disease and cardiovascular disease. Quitting smoking is crucial for improving overall health and reducing the risk of complications. Support from healthcare professionals, nicotine replacement therapies, and behavioral interventions can aid in smoking cessation.

5. **Regular Exercise:** Engaging in regular physical activity has numerous benefits for individuals with kidney disease. Exercise helps control blood pressure, manage weight, improve cardiovascular health, and reduce stress. It is important to consult with a healthcare professional before starting an exercise program to ensure it is safe and appropriate for individual circumstances.

6. **Medication Management:** Proper management of medications is essential for individuals with CKD. It is important to take prescribed medications as directed and communicate any concerns or side effects to the healthcare team. Some medications may need to be adjusted or avoided in the presence of kidney disease.

7. **Stress Management:** Chronic kidney disease can be emotionally and mentally challenging. Stress management techniques, such as relaxation exercises, meditation, and counseling, can help individuals cope with the emotional impact of kidney disease and reduce the risk of cardiovascular complications.

Bone and Mineral Disorders

When you have chronic kidney disease (CKD), your kidneys are not able to function properly, which can lead to a variety of complications throughout your body. One of these complications is the development of bone and mineral disorders. In this section, we will explore the impact of CKD on your bones and minerals, as well as strategies to manage and prevent these disorders.

Understanding Bone and Mineral Disorders

Healthy kidneys play a crucial role in maintaining the balance of minerals, such as calcium and phosphorus, in your body. They help activate vitamin D, which is essential for the absorption of calcium from your diet. Additionally, the kidneys regulate the levels of parathyroid hormone (PTH), which controls the balance of calcium and phosphorus in your bones.

In CKD, impaired kidney function disrupts these processes, leading to imbalances in calcium, phosphorus, and PTH levels.

As a result, several bone and mineral disorders can occur, including:

1. **Renal osteodystrophy:** This condition refers to a group of bone diseases that occur as a result of CKD. It includes osteitis fibrosa cystica, osteomalacia, and a dynamic bone disease. Renal osteodystrophy can cause bone pain, fractures, and deformities.

2. **Secondary hyperparathyroidism:** When the kidneys are unable to regulate PTH levels, it can lead to an overproduction of this hormone. Excessive PTH levels can cause the release of calcium from your bones, leading to weakened bones and an increased risk of fractures.

3. **Vascular calcification:** In CKD, calcium can accumulate in blood vessels, leading to the formation of calcifications. This can impair blood flow and increase the risk of cardiovascular complications.

Managing Bone and Mineral Disorders

Managing bone and mineral disorders in CKD requires a comprehensive approach that focuses on maintaining the balance of minerals, promoting bone health, and preventing complications. Here are some strategies to help you manage these disorders effectively:

1. Diet and Nutrition

A kidney-friendly diet plays a crucial role in managing bone and mineral disorders. It is important to work with a registered dietitian who specializes in CKD to develop a personalized meal plan. Some key dietary considerations include:

- **Phosphorus restriction:** Limiting phosphorus intake is essential to prevent the buildup of this mineral in your blood. This involves avoiding high-phosphorus foods such as dairy products, nuts, and processed foods.

- **Calcium supplementation:** Since CKD can lead to decreased calcium absorption, your doctor may recommend calcium supplements to ensure you meet your daily requirements. However, it is important to take these supplements as directed, as excessive calcium intake can have adverse effects.

- **Vitamin D supplementation:** In CKD, the kidneys may not be able to activate vitamin D properly. Your doctor may prescribe vitamin D supplements to help maintain adequate levels and promote calcium absorption.

2. Medications

In some cases, medications may be prescribed to manage bone and mineral disorders. These medications aim to regulate calcium, phosphorus, and PTH levels. Common medications used include:

- **Phosphate binders:** These medications help prevent the absorption of dietary phosphorus in the digestive tract, reducing its levels in the blood.
- **Calcimimetics:** Calcimimetics mimics the action of calcium on the parathyroid glands, helping to lower PTH levels.
- **Vitamin D analogs:** These medications are synthetic forms of vitamin D that can help regulate calcium and phosphorus levels.

It is important to take these medications as prescribed and to follow up regularly with your healthcare team to monitor their effectiveness and adjust the dosage if needed.

3. Exercise and Physical Activity

Regular exercise and physical activity can have numerous benefits for bone health. Weight-bearing exercises, such as walking or dancing, can help strengthen your bones and reduce the risk of fractures. Additionally, exercise can improve muscle strength and balance, which can further prevent falls and injuries.

However, it is important to consult with your healthcare team before starting any exercise program, as they can provide guidance based on your specific condition and limitations.

4. Monitoring and Prevention

Regular monitoring of your bone and mineral levels is essential to detecting any imbalances or complications early on. Your healthcare team will perform blood tests to assess your calcium, phosphorus, and PTH levels. They may also recommend bone density scans to evaluate your bone health and detect any signs of osteoporosis or fractures.

Prevention is key to managing bone and mineral disorders. By following your prescribed treatment plan, adhering to a kidney-friendly diet, taking medications as directed, and maintaining a healthy lifestyle, you can minimize the risk of complications and promote optimal bone health.

Managing Diabetes and Kidney Disease

Diabetes and kidney disease often go hand in hand. Diabetes is the leading cause of chronic kidney disease (CKD) worldwide. If you have diabetes, it's crucial to understand how it can affect your kidneys and what steps you can take to manage both conditions effectively.

The Link Between Diabetes and Kidney Disease

Diabetes is a condition that affects the body's ability to regulate blood sugar levels. Over time, high blood sugar levels can damage the blood vessels in the kidneys, leading to kidney disease. This condition is known as diabetic nephropathy.

When the kidneys are damaged, they may not function properly, resulting in a buildup of waste and fluid in the body. This can lead to various complications, including high blood pressure, anemia, bone and mineral disorders, and cardiovascular disease.

Controlling Blood Sugar Levels

One of the most important aspects of managing diabetes and kidney disease is controlling blood sugar levels. By keeping your blood sugar within a target range, you can help slow down the progression of kidney disease and reduce the risk of complications.

To control your blood sugar levels effectively, it's essential to follow a diabetes management plan recommended by your healthcare provider. This plan may include:

1. **Monitoring blood sugar:** Regularly checking your blood sugar levels using a glucose meter can help you understand how different foods, medications, and activities affect your blood sugar. This information can guide you in making the necessary adjustments to your diabetes management plan.

2. **Eating a balanced diet:** Following a kidney-friendly diet that is also suitable for diabetes can help you maintain stable blood sugar levels. Focus on consuming whole grains, lean proteins, fruits, vegetables, and healthy fats. Limit your intake of

processed foods, sugary beverages, and high-sodium foods.

3. **Taking diabetes medications:** Your healthcare provider may prescribe medications to help control your blood sugar levels. It's important to take these medications as prescribed and discuss any concerns or side effects with your healthcare team.

4. **Engaging in regular physical activity:** Exercise can help improve insulin sensitivity and lower blood sugar levels. Aim for at least 150 minutes of moderate-intensity aerobic activity, such as brisk walking or cycling, per week. Consult with your healthcare provider before starting any exercise program.

5. **Managing stress:** Stress can affect blood sugar levels, so finding healthy ways to manage stress is crucial. Consider incorporating relaxation techniques, such as deep breathing exercises, meditation, or yoga, into your daily routine.

Kidney Disease Management for Diabetics

In addition to controlling blood sugar levels, there are specific strategies to manage kidney disease in individuals with diabetes. These strategies include:

1. **Managing blood pressure:** High blood pressure can further damage the kidneys. It's important to monitor

and control your blood pressure through lifestyle modifications and medications, if necessary. Follow a low-sodium diet, limit alcohol consumption, maintain a healthy weight, and take prescribed blood pressure medications as directed.

2. **Monitoring kidney function:** Regular monitoring of kidney function through blood and urine tests is essential for individuals with diabetes and kidney disease. These tests can help detect any changes in kidney function and guide treatment decisions.

3. **Managing cholesterol levels:** High cholesterol levels can increase the risk of cardiovascular disease, which is already elevated in individuals with diabetes and kidney disease. Follow a heart-healthy diet, exercise regularly, and take prescribed cholesterol-lowering medications, if necessary.

4. **Controlling protein intake:** In advanced stages of kidney disease, it may be necessary to limit protein intake to reduce the workload on the kidneys. Work with a registered dietitian to determine the appropriate amount of protein for your individual needs.

5. **Avoiding nephrotoxic medications:** Some medications, such as nonsteroidal anti-inflammatory drugs (NSAIDs), can be harmful to the kidneys. Consult with your healthcare provider before taking any over-the-counter medications or supplements.

Collaborating with Your Healthcare Team

Managing both diabetes and kidney disease requires a collaborative approach involving various healthcare professionals. Your healthcare team may include:

- **Primary care physician:** Oversees your overall health and coordinates your care.
- **Endocrinologist:** Specializes in the management of diabetes.
- **Nephrologist:** Specializes in the treatment of kidney diseases.
- **Registered dietitian:** Guides kidney-friendly and diabetes-friendly diets.
- **Diabetes educator:** Offers education and support for managing diabetes.
- **Pharmacist:** Assists in managing medications and addressing any concerns or side effects.

Regular communication with your healthcare team is essential. Be sure to attend all scheduled appointments, ask questions, and discuss any changes in your symptoms or overall health.

Infections and Kidney Disease

Infections can pose a significant risk to individuals with chronic kidney disease (CKD). The compromised immune system and reduced kidney function make it harder for the body to fight off infections, leading to more severe and prolonged illness. Individuals with CKD must take extra precautions to prevent infections and seek prompt medical attention if they suspect an infection.

Common Infections in CKD

There are several types of infections that individuals with CKD are more susceptible to:

1. **Urinary Tract Infections (UTIs):** UTIs are one of the most common infections in individuals with CKD. Reduced kidney function can lead to the accumulation of bacteria in the urinary tract, increasing the risk of infection. Symptoms of UTIs include frequent urination, pain or burning during urination, cloudy or bloody urine, and lower abdominal pain.

2. **Respiratory Infections:** Individuals with CKD are more prone to respiratory infections such as pneumonia and bronchitis. These infections can be more severe and may require hospitalization. Symptoms include coughing, shortness of breath, chest pain, fever, and fatigue.

3. **Skin and Soft Tissue Infections:** CKD can weaken the skin's protective barrier, making it easier for bacteria to enter and cause infections. Skin infections such as cellulitis and abscesses are more common in individuals with CKD. Symptoms include redness, swelling, warmth, and pain in the affected area.

4. **Bloodstream Infections:** In severe cases, infections can spread to the bloodstream, leading to a condition called sepsis. Sepsis is a life-threatening condition that requires immediate medical attention. Symptoms include a high fever, rapid heart rate, confusion, and difficulty breathing.

Preventing Infections

Prevention is key when it comes to managing infections in individuals with CKD. Here are some essential steps to reduce the risk of infection:

1. **Practice Good Hygiene:** It is important to regularly wash your hands with soap and water for at least 20 seconds. This should be done especially before eating, after using the bathroom, and after being in public places. It is also important to avoid touching your face, eyes, nose, and mouth with unwashed hands.

2. **Stay Up to Date with Vaccinations:** Vaccinations can help prevent certain infections. It is important to stay up-to-date with vaccinations such as the flu vaccine, the pneumonia vaccine, and the hepatitis B vaccine. Consult with your healthcare provider to determine which vaccinations are recommended for you.

3. **Maintain a Clean Environment:** Ensure a clean living space by regularly disinfecting frequently

touched surfaces and avoiding close contact with contagious individuals.

4. **Practice Safe Food Handling:** Follow proper food safety practices to prevent foodborne illnesses. Wash fruits and vegetables thoroughly, cook meat and poultry to the recommended temperatures, and avoid consuming raw or undercooked seafood.

5. **Stay Hydrated:** Drinking an adequate amount of water helps flush out toxins from the body and keeps the urinary tract healthy. Aim to drink enough fluids as recommended by your healthcare provider.

Recognizing and Managing Infections

It is important to be vigilant and recognize the signs of infection early on. If you experience any symptoms of infection, it is crucial to seek medical attention promptly. Your healthcare provider will evaluate your symptoms, perform necessary tests, and prescribe appropriate treatment.

In addition to seeking medical care, there are some general measures you can take to manage infections:

1. **Follow Medication Instructions:** If prescribed antibiotics or other medications, make sure to take them as directed by your healthcare provider. Finish the full course of antibiotics even if you start feeling better to ensure the infection is completely eradicated.

2. **Get Adequate Rest:** Resting allows your body to focus on fighting the infection. Make sure to get enough sleep and avoid overexertion.

3. **Stay Hydrated:** Drinking plenty of fluids helps flush out toxins and supports the immune system. Aim to drink water, herbal teas, and other fluids as recommended by your healthcare provider.

4. **Manage Symptoms:** Over-the-counter medications can help manage symptoms such as fever, pain, and congestion. However, it is important to consult with your healthcare provider before taking any medications, as some may be contraindicated for individuals with CKD.

When to Seek Emergency Medical Care

In some cases, infections can become severe and require immediate medical attention. It is important to be aware of the signs that indicate a need for emergency care:

- High fever (above 101°F or 38.3°C)
- Severe pain or discomfort
- Difficulty breathing or shortness of breath
- Confusion or altered mental state
- Rapid heart rate
- Severe weakness or fatigue
- Uncontrolled vomiting or diarrhea

If you experience any of these symptoms, call emergency services or go to the nearest emergency room immediately.

Infections can be a serious concern for individuals with chronic kidney disease. By practicing good hygiene, taking preventive measures, and seeking prompt medical attention, you can reduce the risk of infections and manage them effectively. Remember to consult with your healthcare provider for personalized advice and guidance on managing infections in the context of your specific condition.

Chapter 6

Support and Resources

Building a Support Network

Living with chronic kidney disease (CKD) can be challenging, both physically and emotionally. It is important to remember that you do not have to face this journey alone. Building a strong support network can provide you with the encouragement, understanding, and resources you need to navigate the complexities of managing CKD. In this section, we will explore the importance of a support network and provide practical tips on how to build one.

The Importance of a Support Network

A support network is a group of individuals who can offer emotional support, practical assistance, and guidance throughout your CKD journey. They can include family members, friends, healthcare professionals, support groups, and online communities. Here are some reasons why building a support network is crucial:

1. **Emotional Support:** Dealing with a chronic illness can be emotionally draining. Having a support network

allows you to share your feelings, fears, and frustrations with people who understand what you are going through. They can provide a listening ear, offer empathy, and help you cope with the emotional challenges of CKD.

2. **Practical Assistance:** Managing CKD often involves making lifestyle changes, adhering to a strict diet, and keeping up with medical appointments. A support network can offer practical assistance, such as helping with meal preparation, transportation to appointments, or even just running errands when you are not feeling well.

3. **Information and Resources:** Your support network can be a valuable source of information and resources. They can share their experiences, provide tips on managing symptoms, and recommend healthcare professionals or treatment options. Additionally, they can help you stay informed about the latest research, advancements, and support services available for CKD patients.

4. **Motivation and Encouragement:** Living with CKD can be challenging, and there may be times when you feel discouraged or overwhelmed. Your support network can provide motivation, encouragement, and reminders of your strength and resilience. They can help you stay positive and focused on your goals.

Building Your Support Network

Now that you understand the importance of a support network, let's explore some practical steps to build one:

1. **Communicate with Your Loved Ones:** Start by reaching out to your family members and close friends. Share your diagnosis, educate them about CKD, and explain how they can support you. Encourage open and honest communication so they understand your needs and concerns.

2. **Join Support Groups:** Consider joining local or online support groups specifically for individuals with CKD. These groups provide a safe space to connect with others who are going through similar experiences. You can share your challenges, learn from others, and gain a sense of belonging and understanding.

3. **Attend Educational Programs:** Many hospitals and healthcare organizations offer educational programs and workshops for CKD patients. These programs provide valuable information about managing the disease and offer opportunities to connect with healthcare professionals and other patients.

4. **Utilize Online Communities:** The internet offers a wealth of resources and online communities for CKD patients. Joining forums, social media groups, or online platforms dedicated to kidney disease can

connect you with individuals who can relate to your experiences and provide support and advice.

5. **Seek Professional Support:** In addition to your support network of family and friends, consider seeking professional support. A therapist or counselor can help you navigate the emotional challenges of CKD and provide coping strategies to improve your overall well-being.

6. **Engage with Healthcare Professionals:** Your healthcare team, including doctors, nurses, and dietitians, can be an essential part of your support network. Establish open lines of communication, ask questions, and seek their guidance on managing your condition effectively.

7. **Be Open to New Connections:** Building a support network is an ongoing process. Be open to meeting new people who can offer support and understanding. Attend local events, fundraisers, or awareness campaigns related to kidney disease. You may find individuals who share your experiences and can become valuable additions to your support network.

Remember, building a support network takes time and effort. Be patient with yourself and others as you navigate this journey together. Surrounding yourself with a strong support system can make a significant difference in your ability to manage CKD and maintain a positive outlook on life.

Financial Assistance and Insurance

Managing chronic renal failure can be a challenging and expensive journey. The cost of medications, treatments, and regular doctor visits can quickly add up, placing a significant financial burden on individuals and their families. However, there are resources and options available to help alleviate some of these financial pressures. In this section, we will explore various avenues for financial assistance and discuss the importance of having adequate insurance coverage.

Understanding the Costs

Before diving into financial assistance options, it's crucial to have a clear understanding of the costs associated with managing chronic kidney disease. These costs can vary depending on factors such as the stage of the disease, treatment options, and individual circumstances. Some common expenses include:

1. **Medical appointments:** Regular visits to nephrologists, specialists, and other healthcare professionals are necessary to monitor and manage the disease. These appointments may involve consultation fees, laboratory tests, and imaging studies.
2. **Medications:** Chronic kidney disease often requires a combination of medications to control blood pressure, manage anemia, and address other related conditions.

These medications can be costly, especially if they are not covered by insurance.

3. **Dialysis or transplantation:** For individuals in the advanced stages of chronic kidney disease, dialysis or transplantation may be necessary. Both options come with their own set of expenses, including the cost of the procedure, ongoing treatments, and medications.

4. **Lifestyle modifications:** Making necessary lifestyle changes, such as following a kidney-friendly diet and engaging in regular physical activity, can also incur additional costs. This may include purchasing specialized foods, hiring a dietitian, or joining a gym or exercise program.

Financial Assistance Programs

Fortunately, there are several financial assistance programs available to help individuals with chronic kidney disease manage their expenses. These programs can provide support in various forms, including:

1. **Medicare:** Medicare is a federal health insurance program that provides coverage for individuals aged 65 and older, as well as those with certain disabilities. It plays a crucial role in covering the costs of dialysis and kidney transplantation for eligible individuals.

2. **Medicaid:** Medicaid is a joint federal and state program that provides health coverage to low-income

individuals and families. Eligibility criteria vary by state, but individuals with chronic kidney disease may qualify for Medicaid based on their income and medical needs.

3. **Social Security Disability Insurance (SSDI):** SSDI provides financial assistance to individuals who are unable to work due to a disability, including chronic kidney disease. To qualify, individuals must have a work history and meet specific medical criteria.

4. **Supplemental Security Income (SSI):** SSI is a needs-based program that provides financial assistance to individuals with limited income and resources. It can be particularly helpful for individuals who do not qualify for SSDI but still require financial support.

5. **Patient Assistance Programs (PAPs):** Many pharmaceutical companies offer PAPs to provide free or discounted medications to individuals who meet specific eligibility criteria. These programs can be a valuable resource for individuals struggling to afford their medications.

6. **Nonprofit organizations:** There are numerous nonprofit organizations dedicated to supporting individuals with chronic kidney disease. These organizations may offer financial assistance, educational resources, and support services to help

individuals navigate the challenges of managing the disease.

Insurance Coverage

In addition to financial assistance programs, having adequate insurance coverage is essential for managing chronic kidney disease. Here are some key points to consider:

1. **Health insurance:** It is crucial to have comprehensive health insurance coverage that includes regular check-ups, medications, and treatments related to chronic kidney disease. If you are employed, check with your employer to understand the coverage options available to you. If you are not employed or your employer does not offer health insurance, explore options such as Medicaid or the Health Insurance Marketplace.

2. **Prescription drug coverage:** Ensure that your health insurance plan includes coverage for the medications you need to manage your condition. If your plan does not provide adequate coverage, consider exploring Medicare Part D or prescription assistance programs offered by pharmaceutical companies.

3. **Supplemental insurance:** Supplemental insurance plans, such as Medigap or Medicare Advantage plans, can help cover the gaps in Medicare coverage. These plans may provide additional benefits, such as

coverage for prescription drugs and vision, dental, and hearing services.

4. **Disability insurance:** If you are still working and have not yet developed end-stage renal disease, consider obtaining disability insurance. This type of insurance can provide income replacement if you are unable to work due to your condition.

5. **Life insurance:** While not directly related to managing the costs of chronic kidney disease, having life insurance can provide financial security for your loved ones in the event of your passing. It can help cover funeral expenses and provide financial support for your family.

Remember, it is essential to review and understand the terms and coverage of any insurance policy before making a decision. Consider consulting with an insurance professional or a patient advocate who can guide you through the process and help you make informed choices.

Finding Reliable Information and Resources

When it comes to managing chronic kidney disease (CKD), having access to reliable information and resources is crucial. With the right knowledge and support, you can make informed decisions about your treatment, lifestyle modifications, and overall well-being. In this section, we will explore various sources of reliable information and resources that can help you navigate the challenges of living with CKD.

Healthcare Professionals

Your healthcare team, including your primary care physician, nephrologist, and other specialists, are invaluable sources of information and guidance. They have the expertise and experience to provide you with accurate and up-to-date information about your condition. Don't hesitate to ask questions and seek clarification on any aspect of your kidney disease. Your healthcare professionals can help you understand your test results, explain treatment options, and address any concerns you may have.

National Kidney Foundations and Associations

National kidney foundations and associations are dedicated to supporting individuals with kidney disease and their families. These organizations provide a wealth of information on CKD, including its causes, symptoms, treatment options, and lifestyle recommendations. They often have comprehensive websites with educational materials, fact sheets, and resources that can help you better understand and manage your condition.

Additionally, national kidney foundations and associations may offer support groups, educational events, and helplines staffed by trained professionals. These resources can provide you with emotional support, connect you with others who are going through similar experiences, and offer practical advice on coping with the challenges of CKD.

Online Resources

The internet can be a valuable tool for finding information about CKD, but it's important to be cautious and ensure that the sources you rely on are reputable and trustworthy. Look for websites that are run by reputable medical institutions, government agencies, or well-known health organizations. These websites often provide evidence-based information, research updates, and practical tips for managing CKD.

Some reliable online resources for kidney disease include:

- National Institute of Diabetes and Digestive and Kidney Diseases (NIDDK)
- American Kidney Fund (AKF)
- National Kidney Foundation (NKF)
- Mayo Clinic
- WebMD

Remember to critically evaluate the information you find online and consult with your healthcare team if you have any doubts or questions.

Books and Publications

Books and publications written by reputable authors and healthcare professionals can provide in-depth knowledge and insights into managing CKD. Look for books that are specifically focused on kidney disease and written in a language that is accessible and easy to understand. These resources can help you gain a deeper understanding of your condition, treatment options, and lifestyle modifications.

Some recommended books on kidney disease include:

- "Living Well with Kidney Disease" by the National Kidney Foundation
- "Kidney Disease: A Guide for Living" by Walter A. Hunt
- "The Kidney Disease Solution" by Duncan Capicchiano
- "Kidney Health Gourmet Diet Guide & Cookbook" by Nina Kolbe

Support Groups and Online Communities

Connecting with others who are going through similar experiences can be incredibly helpful in managing CKD. Support groups and online communities provide a safe space to share your concerns, ask questions, and learn from others who have firsthand experience with kidney disease. These groups can offer emotional support, practical advice, and a sense of community.

You can find local support groups through national kidney foundations, hospitals, or community centers. Online communities, such as forums and social media groups, can also provide a platform for connecting with others virtually. However, always remember to prioritize your privacy and be cautious about sharing personal information online.

Educational Programs and Workshops

Many healthcare institutions, kidney foundations, and community organizations offer educational programs and workshops for individuals with CKD. These programs cover a wide range of topics, including nutrition, medication management, coping strategies, and self-care. Attending these programs can provide you with valuable information, practical skills, and an opportunity to connect with healthcare professionals and other individuals living with kidney disease.

Check with your healthcare team, local hospitals, and kidney foundations for information on upcoming educational programs and workshops in your area.

Your Personal Network

Don't underestimate the power of your personal network to find reliable information and resources. Reach out to friends, family members, or colleagues who may have experience with or knowledge about kidney disease. They may be able to provide recommendations for healthcare professionals, share helpful tips, or connect you with relevant support groups or resources.

Remember, while your personal network can be a valuable source of support, always consult with your healthcare team for medical advice and treatment decisions.

Your Healthcare Team

Lastly, never hesitate to reach out to your healthcare team if you have any questions or concerns about the information you find or the resources you come across. They are there to support you and can help you navigate through the vast amount of information available.

By utilizing these reliable sources of information and resources, you can empower yourself to take an active role in managing your chronic kidney disease. Remember, knowledge is power, and with the right information and support, you can make informed decisions that positively impact your health and well-being.

Advocacy and Patient Rights

Advocacy and understanding your rights as a patient are crucial aspects of managing chronic kidney disease (CKD). As you navigate through the challenges of this condition, it's important to be aware of the resources and support available to you. This section will provide you with valuable information on advocacy and patient rights, empowering you to take an active role in your healthcare journey.

Understanding Advocacy

Advocacy involves speaking up for yourself and others, ensuring that your needs and concerns are heard and addressed. When it comes to managing CKD, advocacy plays a vital role in ensuring that you receive the best possible care and support. Here are some key aspects of advocacy to consider:

1. Self-Advocacy

Self-advocacy is the ability to express your needs, concerns, and preferences regarding your healthcare. As a patient with CKD, it's important to become your own advocate by:

- **Educating yourself about your condition:** The more you know about CKD, its treatment options, and potential complications, the better equipped you'll be to make informed decisions about your care.
- **Asking questions:** Don't hesitate to ask your healthcare team questions about your treatment plan, medications, and any concerns you may have. Remember, you have the right to understand and be involved in your own healthcare decisions.
- **Communicating effectively:** Clearly express your symptoms, concerns, and preferences to your healthcare team. Effective communication is key to receiving the care you need.

2. Support Networks

Building a strong support network is an essential part of advocacy. Surrounding yourself with individuals who understand and support you can provide emotional and practical assistance. Consider the following sources of support:

- **Family and friends:** Lean on your loved ones for emotional support and assistance with daily tasks when needed.
- **Support groups:** Joining a support group for individuals with CKD can provide a sense of community and the opportunity to share experiences and advice.
- **Online communities:** Participating in online forums and communities dedicated to CKD can connect you with individuals who are going through similar experiences.

3. Healthcare Team Collaboration

Collaborating with your healthcare team is crucial for effective advocacy. By working together, you can ensure that your treatment plan aligns with your goals and preferences. Here are some tips for collaborating with your healthcare team:

- **Be proactive:** Take an active role in your healthcare by asking questions, expressing your concerns, and actively participating in your treatment decisions.

- **Seek second opinions:** If you're unsure about a diagnosis or treatment plan, don't hesitate to seek a second opinion from another healthcare professional.
- **Keep records:** Maintain a record of your medical history, test results, and medications. This will help you stay organized and provide accurate information to your healthcare team.

Patient Rights

Understanding your rights as a patient is essential for advocating for yourself and ensuring that you receive appropriate care. Familiarize yourself with the following patient rights:

1. **Informed Consent:** As a patient, you have the right to be fully informed about your treatment options, potential risks, and benefits. Before undergoing any medical procedure or starting a new treatment, your healthcare provider should explain the details and obtain your informed consent.
2. **Access to Medical Records:** You have the right to access your medical records and request copies. Reviewing your medical records can help you understand your condition better and ensure that the information is accurate.
3. **Confidentiality and Privacy:** Your healthcare information should be kept confidential and shared

only with individuals involved in your care. You have the right to privacy during medical examinations and discussions.

4. **Right to Refuse Treatment:** You have the right to refuse any treatment or procedure. However, it's important to have open discussions with your healthcare team to fully understand the potential consequences of refusing recommended treatments.

5. **Complaints and Grievances:** If you have concerns or complaints about your healthcare experience, you have the right to voice them. Most healthcare facilities have a formal process for addressing complaints and grievances. Contact the appropriate department or patient advocate to initiate the process.

6. **Access to Information:** You have the right to access information about your condition, treatment options, and potential risks. Your healthcare team should provide you with clear and understandable explanations to help you make informed decisions.

Advocacy Resources

To further support your advocacy efforts, consider utilizing the following resources:

- **Patient advocacy organizations:** Many organizations specialize in supporting patients with CKD. They can provide valuable information, resources, and support.

Examples include the National Kidney Foundation and the American Association of Kidney Patients.

- **Social workers:** Hospital social workers can assist you in navigating the healthcare system, connecting you with resources, and addressing any concerns you may have.

- **Patient advocacy programs:** Some hospitals and healthcare systems offer patient advocacy programs that provide guidance and support throughout your healthcare journey.

Remember, advocacy is an ongoing process. By staying informed, building a support network, and understanding your rights, you can actively participate in your healthcare decisions and ensure that your needs are met.

Conclusion

The kidney disease journey presents many uncertainties and challenges. But with the right outlook and support, you can continue pursuing a fulfilling life despite the diagnosis. This book has equipped you with extensive information to better understand chronic kidney disease and make informed decisions about your treatment options.

More importantly, you now have the tools to take an active role in managing your health every day. From dietary guidelines to home care routines, use the tips in this handbook to create stability through your changing kidney function. Track your lab results, nourish your body, and celebrate small victories like learning a new low-potassium recipe.

Surround yourself with a diverse support network, whether that's loved ones, a community group, or an online forum. Don't underestimate the power of sharing experiences and finding camaraderie. You are not alone on this journey.

Finally, don't forget the importance of maintaining emotional strength. Adjusting your mindset, managing stress, and focusing on positivity can make the hard days easier. Appreciate life's simple joys, adapt as needed, and believe in your ability to thrive with kidney disease.

This is not an end, but rather a new phase in your life's journey—one that can be fulfilled despite the challenges. Use this book as an invaluable reference and guide. Keep putting one foot in front of the other with courage and hope. The future is still yours to embrace.